Construction Managemen

2

Management Systems

CONSTRUCTION TECHNOLOGY AND MANAGEMENT

A series published in association with the Chartered Institute of Building.

This series will, when complete, cover every important aspect of construction. It will be of particular relevance to the needs of students taking the CIOB Member Examinations, Parts 1 and 2, but will also be suitable for degree courses, other professional examinations, and practitioners in building, architecture, surveying and related fields.

Project Evaluation and Development
Alexander Rougvie

Practical Building Law
Margaret Wilkie with Richard Howells

Building Technology (3 volumes)
Ian Chandler
    Vol. 1 Site Organisation and Method
    Vol. 2 Performance
    Vol. 3 Design, Production and Maintenance

The Economics of the Construction Industry
Geoffrey Briscoe

Construction Management (2 volumes)
Robert Newcombe, David Langford and Richard Fellows
    Vol. 1 Organisation Systems
    Vol. 2 Management Systems

CONSTRUCTION MANAGEMENT

2

Management Systems

Robert Newcombe
David Langford
Richard Fellows

Mitchell · London

in association with the Chartered Institute of Building

© Robert Newcombe, David Langford and Richard Fellows 1990
First published 1990

All rights reserved. No part of this publication
may be reproduced, in any form or by any means,
without permission from the Publisher

Typeset by Deltatype Ltd, Ellesmere Port
and printed in Great Britain by
Dotesios Printers Ltd, Trowbridge, Wilts

Published by The Mitchell Publishing Company Limited
4 Fitzhardinge Street, London W1H 0AH
A subsidiary of B T Batsford Limited

A CIP catalogue record for this book is
available from the British Library

ISBN 0 7134 6534 4

Contents

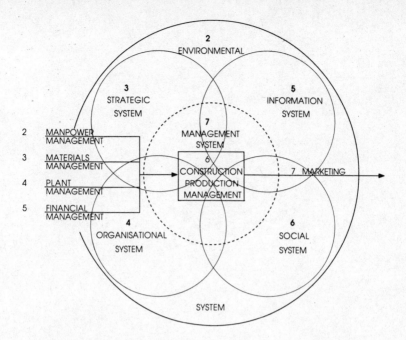

Figures in **bold** type above refer to chapters in Volume 1, those in light type to chapters in this volume.

This volume should be read in conjunction with Volume 1. Chapter 1 contains a summary of the main ideas from the first chapter of Volume 1, to which reference should be made for a fuller exposition.

1 Systems Concepts

1.1 Introduction

Volume 2 of *Construction Management* addresses the systems which are used to manage the building process. The material covered introduces key resources to be used by construction organisations.* Put alliteratively they are the four Ms of construction organisation, *Men*, *Money*, *Machines* and *Material*. Chapters 2 to 5 in this volume cover the management of these key inputs to construction organisations. The treatment of these topics will not be exhaustive but will attempt to distill existing research and practice within the systems context. These are inputs which any construction organisation must obtain to ensure survival.

Chapter 6 is concerned with the core of all construction organisations – the construction production process which converts inputs into outputs. As with inputs, a 'strategic' rather than 'operational' view of this process will be adopted. The nature of the construction production process will be examined from first principles and the implications for managing the process both centrally and at site level will be analysed.

The last chapter is concerned with the critical (but only recently recognised) function of marketing the outputs of the construction organisation. Again, the treatment will not be exhaustive but rather present an overview of the theory and practice of marketing within the construction environment described in chapter 2. Whilst a substantial body of theory exists about marketing products, the majority of it is not relevant to construction organisations; a selective approach is therefore essential.

The framework for considering Volume 2 of *Construction Management* is again the systems approach. It will be recalled that Volume 1 explains in detail the concepts of Systems Theory and how it can be applied to organisations, and particularly those related to the construction industry. It addresses construction organisation systems and uses the model shown in figure 1.1 as a starting point for analysing the strategic, information, organisational, and management systems which dominate construction organisations.

---

* Please note that throughout both volumes of this book, the term 'construction organisations' refers to both building and civil engineering firms.

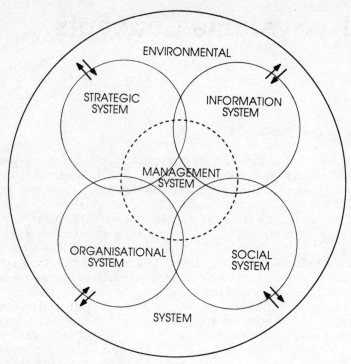

1.1   Construction organisation systems

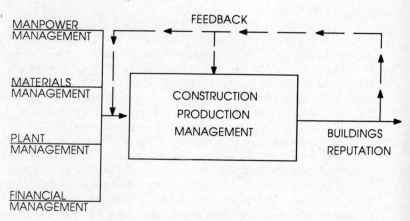

1.2   Input-conversion – output model

This framework is overlaid with an input–conversion–output process which is used to analyse the management systems which are discussed in this volume. Figure 1.2 illustrates the input–conversion–output model and figure 1.3 extends this to

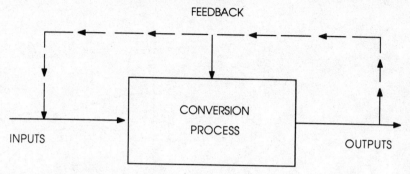

1.3 Construction management systems

accommodate the particular chapters incorporated in this volume. By overlaying figure 1.1 and 1.3 we can produce a composite systems model of the construction organisation as shown in figure 1.4.

1.2 The systems approach

Like Volume 1 this book sees Systems Theory as a powerful tool for analysing construction organisations. Volume 1 defined the characteristics of a system and it will be recalled that Systems Theory uses inter-related sub-systems to pursue goals or objectives. The starting point of Systems Theory is to define a *Primary Task*; that which an organisation must do to survive. It is worth re-stating some important systems concepts to assist in the comprehension of this text.

Systems concepts include:

(a) That large systems are comprised of smaller sub-systems which work, preferably independently, towards the larger systems goals or Primary Task.

(b) That those sub-systems form a hierarchy of systems and by studying the inter-relationships of the sub-systems, we can understand the larger system.

(c) That systems are 'open' because they interact with their environment. The environment affects the systems through constraints and imperatives but is not a part of the system because it does not share the goals of the system.

(d) That the system receives inputs from the environment, applies some sort of conversion process and exports outputs to the environment.

(e) That there is a permeable boundary between the system and its environment through which inputs and outputs pass. 'Boundary Management', or managing the interface between

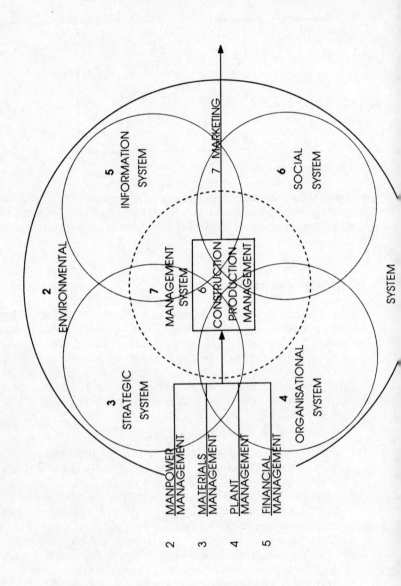

1.4   A systems model of the construction organisation

the system and its environment is a key systems concept. These boundary management positions are usually very stressful. Boundaries also occur between sub-systems within a larger system.

(f) That there is feedback when part of the output is fed back to become an input; thus a cycle of events is established which enables the system to monitor its own behaviour.

Having recorded these characteristics it must be said that Systems Theory is more than just a set of concepts. The Open University (1974) see 'systems' as a 'way of thinking'.

'. . . the systems approach is a way of thinking which enables us to cope with complex phenomena by identifying their systemic relations. Once we realise that the structure we are studying displays the properties of a system we may be in a position to identify crucial goals, linkages or controlling factors in its structure and functioning. The analytical process typical of systems analysis can lay bare the inter-relationships between sub-systems and their inputs and outputs, and may focus our attention on unexpected feedback loops, behavioural lags, delays in response to particular inputs, or crucial interactions between inputs or sub-systems. The systems concept ensures that we look for these linkages since we are aware that the structure we are studying is an independent arrangement of sub-systems.'

This 'way of thinking' epitomises the approach of this book to the study of construction organisations.

So the systems approach is a way of thinking about organisations which uses the following procedures:

1   *Define the system.* This is done in two ways:
    (a)   a description of what the system is and what it does – the Primary Task;
    (b)   the establishing of the boundary of the system – what is inside and what is outside the system.

2   *Identify the component parts of the system:*
    (a)   the inputs to the system;
    (b)   the conversion processes which the system uses to transform the inputs into outputs;
    (c)   the outputs of the system, both tangible and intangible;
    (d)   the feedback loops which complete the input-conversion–output cycle.

3   *Define the environment of the system*, ie what is outside the system in terms of which elements impact on the system and vice-versa. The environment will consist of other organisational systems

and the general environment. It is an understanding of the interactions of these systems which is the essence of systems thinking. The following section and the subsequent chapters will adopt this pattern of analysis.

1.3   Construction management systems

It follows from this definition of the Primary Task that the dominant input–conversion–output process is centred on the construction site. At the heart of a construction organisation is the building site. Therefore *construction production* is the dominant *conversion process* performed by building firms. Characteristic of the industry is that this process is unique, temporary and dispersed to a number of geographically decentralised sites. The majority of the process is exposed to the climatic elements and conducted by teams especially assembled for the purpose. These multi-disciplinary teams are often from independent organisations, which led the Tavistock Institute (1966) to describe the nature of the relationship within the building team as one of 'interdependent autonomy'. The character of the conversion process creates a high degree of technical and social uncertainty amongst the parties involved so that *interdependence* and *uncertainty* are key features of the construction production process (Tavistock 1966). The dominant *inputs* to this process are human, physical and financial. Construction is a people centred and dominated industry whose craft processes and management practices have changed slowly.

The nature of the process just described means that mass production techniques or even robotics are unlikely to find wide-scale applications on building sites. People will be a prime, and increasingly scarce, resource for construction activity for the foreseeable future.

The construction process is an assembly process requiring *physical inputs* in the form of materials and components. The materials and components are often bulky and heavy and whilst, in the past, large numbers of people were used to achieve remarkable feats of building, today the shortage of people has led to the development of sophisticated plant to carry out the heaviest tasks. The domination of the skyline of a construction site by a tower crane is a relatively recent phenomenon as is the use of mechanical excavators and concrete mixers. The point is that these machines are able to achieve previously unattainable levels of production but at a cost. They are expensive to buy and operate, even more expensive when they are *not* operating. The skilful management of plant both on and off the building site is crucial to the success of the modern building project. Building requires large capital investment and the flow of *financial inputs* to the business is critical to the survival of the building firm. Very few building firms can afford to fund the construction of buildings and rely on making contracts with clients in which the client will provide the main financial input. This input is usually made in stage payments against the physical progress of the project so that financial management skills of a high order are essential to ensure adequate cash flow to maintain the business. This financial flow is one of the key feedback components generated by the outputs of the building conversion process.

Within a growing construction organisation the early differentiation by function described earlier centres on the creation of *Personnel*, *Materials*, *Plant* and *Financial Management* roles to manage the human, physical and financial inputs to the business.

Given the Primary Task of the construction organisation described previously the tangible *outputs* of the construction conversion process are buildings and related facilities. The *Marketing* of these outputs is therefore a primary function of the building contractor. Again, a characteristic of the industry is that the product, ie the building, is usually sold before it is produced which makes traditional marketing techniques, designed for the selling of consumer goods, largely irrelevant. These marketing techniques are appropriate for certain sectors of the industry, eg speculative housebuilding, but for the general building contractor constructing custom designed building there is little opportunity to market a product. It is, in fact, the intangible package of building skills which is the real output of the building firm. The physical output of the conversion process is a building but the building contractor is really marketing the skills of planning and marshalling the resources (or inputs), and managing the conversion process to a successful concluson. Effective marketing forms a feedback loop again to enable the firm to obtain new contracts requiring fresh human, physical and financial inputs thus maintaining the production cycle and the steady state of the firm. This input–conversion–output process with the tangible resources used in construction provide the substance of this book.

2 The Manpower Sub-system

2.1 Introduction

In Volume 1 of this text we saw how a central task of a building organisation was to formulate a corporate strategy. This strategy was not developed in isolation from the resources which would be necessary to operate the strategy and it was seen that 'people' were central to the 'operationalising' of strategy. Figure 2.1 shows the relationship between the strategic decisions of the organisation, the strategic manpower decisions and the procedures necessary for planning within the context of our organisational plan. Using the systems model, figure 2.1 shows the interaction between the elements of the manpower sub-system.

For the purposes of this chapter the manpower sub-system is said to include directly employed workers; sub-contractors, suppliers, etc, are not included within the sub-system. Moreover, important aspects of the manpower system such as industrial relations, safety, training and the legal framework for employment are not covered. For full treatment of these issues readers should refer to *Construction Management Practice* by Fellows, Langford, Newcombe and Urry (Longmans 1983).

Considering the input – Manpower
It has been noted that the manpower sub-system must be seen in the context of the managerial system and this implies that the corporate strategy of the construction company will drive the nature of the conversion process. The strategic decisions about manpower could

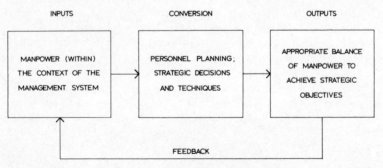

2.1   A systems model of the manpower sub-system

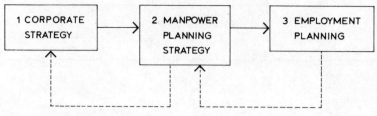

2.2   Strategy and manpower planning

focus upon the number of employees and qualifications required to meet the organisation's objectives within the planning period. Figure 2.2 shows the relationship between some of the issues dominating the managerial sub-system and the people sub-system.

The questions posed in boxes 2 or 3 could be as follows:

Box 2
What are our manpower objectives?
How does the manpower planning and personnel function contribute to this business?
At what stage are we in realising our manpower objectives?
What needs to be done to move from where we are to where we want to be?

Box 3
Based on the firm's objectives, what will be our demand for the various types of manpower that a construction firm is likely to need?
What is the supply of this manpower?
How do we close any gap betwen the supply and the demand?

2.2   Inputs – an overview

Figure 5.1 shows 'Manpower' as the input, but this needs further classification to enable us to analyse the needs of a company. Whilst it is not original nor subtle, it is proposed to break this down into two types of manpower: *Managerial Technical* and *Operative*.

Management and technical inputs
The Housing and Construction Statistics (1987) records the extent of Administrative, Professional, Technical and Clerical (APTC) staffs employed in the building industry as being 220,000 in 1987. It is noticeable that whilst the absolute numbers of such staff has declined in response to the recession of 1978–1983, the proportion

	APTC	Operatives	APTC as a percentage of operatives
1980	235	760	31%
1981	226	659	34%
1982	214	587	36%
1983	214	600	36%
1984	214	585	37%
1985	213	586	36%
1986	212	530	40%
1987 (July)	220	541	41%

Table 2.1   The ratio of APTC staff to operatives

of such staff in the workforce has increased. Table 2.1 charts the growth in the percentage of such persons serving the industry.

What is evident is that there is a greater managerial intensity in the construction industry in the late 1980s – more managerial and technical staff are required to service the declining operative population. Certainly the increased use of subcontractors in the construction end of the business has created demands for co-ordination of work, greater technical sophistication of buildings and different procurement methods have contributed to the growth of the proportion of employees dedicated to this type of employment in the industry.

Operatives
The striking feature of the operative labour force is the apparently contradictory characteristics of turbulence and stability. The labour force may be regarded as being turbulent both in the numbers employed and in the employment arrangements under which it is hired. It may be seen as stable in that the changes in its composition have been minimal in contrast to the change in construction methods, types of procurement and contractual methods which provide the framework for the employment of labour. The figures in table 2.2 demonstrate the point:

The very stability points up the manpower crisis which periodically besets the construction industry: insufficient skilled manpower to service construction demand. These figures are drawn from the Housing and Construction Statistics which record contractors' employment. This of course does not represent the whole picture, sub-contractors will not be included in these returns and it is possible that this is the volatile end of the labour market which is unrecorded. If these are the inputs, what needs to happen to them in the construction organisation if one is to achieve an objective of

	Index of changes in operative workers since 1980	Index of changes in workload since 1980
1980	100	100
1981	96	90.5
1982	91	91.8
1983	91	95.7
1984	91	99
1985	91	100.1
1986	91	102.8
1987	94	111

Table 2.2   Changes in operatives and workload

ensuring human effectiveness? Whilst it is important to note the differences between these grades of employee, it is not intended to treat them differently in the subsequent analysis of the manpower system. The conversion process discussed will attend to principles which can be applied throughout the construction organisation. However, examples will be used which demonstrate applications for both types of employee.

2.3   The conversion process

Before discussing the techniques that may be used to forecast demand for or evaluate sources of manpower in construction, it is necessary to explore some reasons for the necessity of manpower planning in construction. The reasons are not at all obvious for many have argued that in such a volatile market as construction it is not feasible to forecast demand for manpower. Changes in construction technology and materials compound the difficulty in predicting what kind of skills are necessary for the future. These difficulties lead to many construction organisations paying lip service to the idea of manpower planning, yet the difficulties of manpower may lead more and more firms into the area of forward planning. Not least of the reasons for this is the realisation that planning can offer:

- More effective manpower (to paraphrase DRUCKER: 'manpower doing the right things')
- More efficient manpower (again from DRUCKER, manpower 'doing things right')
- Contented manpower (to paraphrase McGREGOR, 'a happy workforce is a productive one').

Taking each in turn; if manpower planning is to ensure that employees are 'doing the right things' then it behoves the organisa-

tion to *select* the staff who are attuned to the organisation's values
and requirements.

For example, the needs of a civil engineering contractor and a
house builder are likely to be different; one may characterise house
building organisations as being very centralised whilst major civils'
projects can afford greater autonomy to the site manager. The
different structures being functions of the product being built by the
companies. The site managers in each organisation may be
expected to behave differently for the 'right thing' to do is different
in each type of company. Therefore manpower planning personal-
ises the needs of the organisation by recruiting the people best able
to fill these needs. Secondly, the manpower sub-system needs to
develop 'efficient' people. Efficiency is not natural, one may have
an aptitude to be an efficient, say, site accountant but unless the
particular procedures are shown to the site accountant then this
aptitude is unlikely to emerge in an 'efficient' performance. So in
order to make manpower efficient then training requirements need
to be assayed. Finally, 'contentedness' needs to be considered. A
well planned manpower system can generate enthusiasm by the
employees (of whatever grade). If people have an opportunity to
participate in their work or career development through training
opportunities then they may be more contented in their jobs with
consequent benefits in terms of better performance, lower
absenteeism, better safety, etc.

Forecasting demand for manpower
FELLOWS *et al.* (1982) reviewed the process of how construction
organisations forecast demand for manpower. The authors argued
that the ad-hoc approach surrounding recruitment from sites added
turbulence and uncertainty to building workers' job prospects.
Equally the top-down approach to manpower forecasts is un-
realistic for organisations such as construction companies which are
largely decentralised organisations. The most effective source of
manpower forecasts is likely to be a combination of the bottom-up
and top-down methods.

Demand forecasting for labour, of whatever grade, is always
more likely to be an art than a science – this aphorism is even more
true in construction than other, more stable, industries. In recognition of this condition, manpower planners must use head and
heart, logic and emotion, to best judge manpower demands.
FELLOWS *et al.* (op cit) presented a model for predicting manpower
demand and the concomitant supply. This model is shown in figure
2.3.

As can be seen from this model, there are two major elements
which have to be quantified; the forecasts for demand and forecasts
for supply.

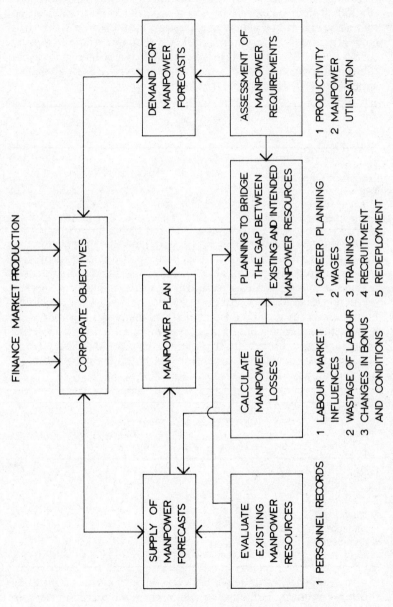

FINANCE   MARKET   PRODUCTION

CORPORATE OBJECTIVES

DEMAND FOR MANPOWER FORECASTS

ASSESSMENT OF MANPOWER REQUIREMENTS

1 PRODUCTIVITY
2 MANPOWER UTILISATION

PLANNING TO BRIDGE THE GAP BETWEEN EXISTING AND INTENDED MANPOWER RESOURCES

1 CAREER PLANNING
2 WAGES
3 TRAINING
4 RECRUITMENT
5 REDEPLOYMENT

MANPOWER PLAN

CALCULATE MANPOWER LOSSES

1 LABOUR MARKET INFLUENCES
2 WASTAGE OF LABOUR
3 CHANGES IN BONUS AND CONDITIONS

SUPPLY OF MANPOWER FORECASTS

EVALUATE EXISTING MANPOWER RESOURCES

1 PERSONNEL RECORDS

2.3   *Manpower planning within corporate objectives*

Manpower forecasts – numbers required

There are many ways of handling this problem. The most simple is by extrapolation. Let us take an example of a construction company with a turnover of £300 m and a site management staff of 150 which includes site managers, engineers, site based planners, etc. It has plans for expansion into a region where it is currently under-represented and hopes that this will increase the turnover by 10% in the next two years. It is not anticipated that the type of work will change nor the work which one person can supervise. This data is tabulated below.

	Current year £m	Plan year estimate £m
Turnover	300	330
Present site managers	150	
Turnover per site manager (pa)	£2	£2
Site managers required		165

One future assumption would be that because the market is moving to a more sophisticated type of structure and this implies that managers are not as able to handle as much volume then assume a 5% decrease in turnover per site manager. Another scenario would be that more 'buildable' designs were becoming more commonplace and this enabled site managers to supervise a greater turnover per unit of time. Assuming a 7% increase on site managers' supervisory 'capacity' then demand could be altered to fit the assumptions, which of course must be based upon the 'strategy' of the company. This data is tabulated below.

	Current year £m	Plan year estimate £m	Planyear estimate with 5% decrease £m	Planyear with 7% increase £m
Turnover	300	330	330	330
Present site managers	150	–	–	–
Turnover per manager	£2	£2	£1.9	£2.07
Site managers required		165	173	161

Other approaches to demand forecasting are more complex but the basic concept remains the same, demand for manpower is generated by turnover. More sophisticated demand forecasting uses quantitative techniques but these require extensive data bases of employment records and operational research analysts to use them. MILKOVITCH and GLUECK (1985) identify techniques which may be used and include the following:

1 *Market analysis*– this technique uses historical data to predict future trends. Data from personnel concerning losses, promotions, retirements, etc, are used to predict future needs.
2 *Simulation* – this adds further sophistication by building in 'what-if' questions. This enables the forecaster to predict manpower requirements under different sets of corporate planning scenarios and external trading conditions.
3 *Renewal analysis* – estimates the flows of personnel due to changes in the organisation and the individual employee preferences. The availability of employees is gauged by the organisational rules governing the filling of vacancies.
4 *Target setting* – this is the mechanism by which establishing targets on such matters of percentage of new recruits, salary budgets per department, etc. This then controls the organisation's growth and development.

Not only will companies need to know the absolute numbers of those it wishes to employ but will need to assess the skills mix. Again FELLOWS *et al.* (op cit) offers a method of analysing the mix within the company. It must be noted here that many construction companies use the same distribution of skills or job type for the next planning period as for the present. Again using construction professionals as an example, the distribution be as shown in table 2.3.

		Current year	%	Plan year forecast	%
		Number		Number	
1	Contracts managers	5	4	7	4
2	Project managers (senior agents)	20	14	24	14
3	Site agents	35	21	37	21
4	Engineers	40	28	48	28
5	Site surveyors	50	33	57	33
		150		173	

Table 2.3 Typical staff distribution by occupation

This pattern of replicating what has gone before assumes that the type of work undertaken by the company will be the same for the planning year as it is for the current year. This may not be so. For example, a shift away from contract work to design and build may depress the need for surveyors but increase new demands for design staff; a shift into refurbishment may enhance the need for surveyors. Again the manpower needs must be driven by the strategy.

The supply side

An analysis of the supply of personnel for the construction organisation must focus upon questions such as:

- What type of people will we need?
- Where can we find them?
- How can we make any necessary adjustments?

The first question is the most difficult. In construction the uncertainty about the overall workload and the proportion that an individual company will obtain makes forecasts of the number of people required difficult. Also the variegation of the type of work undertaken by a building organisation is likely to make estimates of the supply difficult. Nonetheless, if we are to manage the resources effectively then we must try to analyse the skills necessary. To start this process the organisation may undertake some techniques to analysing labour supply. They are *skills inventories* and for managerial and technical *staff replacement and succession charts.*

Skills inventories

Good skills inventories enable management to determine what kinds of people with specific skills are currently available. Such data is useful when new contracts are awarded as well as planning training, promotions, transfers, etc. Designing the skills inventory is critical to its usefulness. For operatives the kind of information would be limited and since a considerable proportion of the workload is sub-contracted the skills inventory of the organisation will need to include internal and external resources. Data for internal resources could include personal details followed by the person's trade and an assessment of the level of skill which the employer exercises, the skill, prior experience, history of work experience in the firm, absenteeism, any plus rates that the person is entitled to, etc. For sub-contractors the inventory is based more on the qualities of the sub-contractor organisation rather than individuals. Data about size (in terms of people), turnover, limitations on the distance that the sub-contractor will travel, quality of work produced, rates paid for previous work, etc, will be useful.

For managerial and technical staff a more comprehensive coverage will be needed. Personal details will need to be supported by information on experience, education, health, knowledge of a foreign language, publications, hobbies, salary/salary range. All of this information must be coupled with the manager or technician's own stated personal goals and preferences. In construction this may revolve around locational preferences.

Such skills inventory data can identify employees for specific contracts or regional offices which not only fulfil the organisational objective but the individual's needs as well. So these skills inventories can be used for long-range personnel planning and development. By defining the skills, aptitudes and interests of current staff the inventory crystalises the needs of the organisation and the development needs of the individuals. It may also uncover imbalances, ie too many surveyors or site engineers, etc, which can lead to personnel problems for the future. Finally the skills inventory can be used as a tool for motivating staff by demonstrating that the organisation has a systematic approach to using such data and is eager to develop each employee.

However, it must be pointed out that data held on computer is subject to the Data Protection Act (1986) and individuals have a right of access to the information held.

Replacement and succession charts
These are devices used to analyse and project the supply of management talent. Such charts are there to identify managers who can expect rapid promotion, those who should expect the normal rate of advance and the small number who are poor performers in their current jobs. The replacement chart looks at the organisation and identifies replacements for managers. Figure 2.4 shows an example.

This process can go down the line and indicate replacement project managers from the surveyors, engineers, etc, serving on a project. This system is not without its critics. For example, any job is changed by the person who holds the job and the replacement chart presumes a 'cloning' effect that the best person to replace is the one which fits the job as it is currently defined and carried out. Also replacement charting may box-in individuals and eliminate visions of horizontal moves, ie the surveyor not moving up the surveying ladder but promoted, say, in administration where his or her abilities may shine. Thirdly the appraisal of replacements may be based upon current performance which may be enhanced by programmes of management development – it can be a static rather than dynamic appraisal.

Another way of taking stock is to develop a matrix of the organisation which can show the percentage of people moving up through the organisation over a period of time. In the example this time period is ten years but any time interval can be used.

Figure 2.5 shows a hierarchy of jobs in a construction organisation. The vertical list is the position in 1979 and the horizontal list as it is in 1989. To use the chart follow the example.

Let us take two examples from this chart. Let us say that there are ten main board members in 1979. By 1989 one has been promoted to Managing Director, one has left the organisation and eight

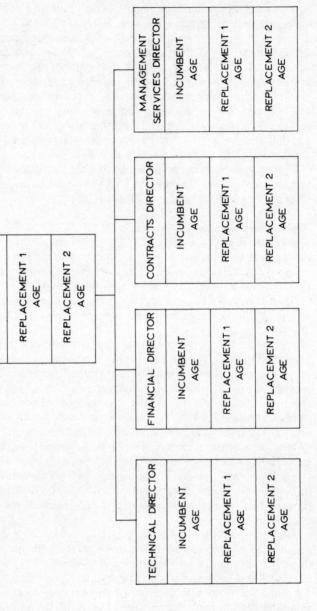

2.4 Replacement chart

		A	B	C	D	E	F	G	H	I	J	EXIT	TOTAL
MANAGING DIRECTOR	A	1.00											
MAIN BOARD MEMBER	B	.10	.80									.10	
REGIONAL DIRECTOR	C	.80		.76	.04							.12	
REGIONAL BOARD MEMBER	D		.01	.23	.73							.03	
CONTRACTS MANAGER/ DEPARTMENT MANAGER	E					.85	.05					.10	
SITE AGENT/ MIDDLE MANAGER	F					.25	.65	.05				.07	
SUB-AGENT/G.F.	G						.40	.50	.03			.07	
SITE ENGINEER/ SURVEYOR	H						.02	.15	.75			.08	
SITE TECHNICIAN	I								.20	.50		.30	
TRADES FOREMAN	J										.50	.50	
RECRUIT					.10				.20	.30	.40		

2.5 *Succession charts*

remain where they were. Moving down the ladder, if there were fifty regional directors in 1979 and four were promoted to the main board by 1989, a further two had been moved down to regional board members and a further three had left the organisation, then forty one will have remained in post over the period. The data is expressed as percentage of 1, eg .08 represents 4 of the 50 Regional Directors promoted to the board. This process can be followed through for each job grade. What can it tell us? Firstly it can identify career paths. For example, it can be seen that no contracts managers/department managers have been promoted to regional board members in the ten years. This may be worrying for the organisation and be leading to considerable frustration amongst the contracts managers. Secondly the chart can show at what grades there needs to be recruitment. Trades foremen turn over quickly; half left the organisation and none moved into being a site technician over the study period. This would suggest that being a trades foreman is a 'dead end' job and high recruitment is required to sustain the post *or* the job changed to afford greater prospects.

How do we recruit the necessary people? (or 'how do we find them?')
It has frequently been said that a construction organisation's central resource is the people they employ. The previous section sought to identify the 'type' of people a company may need, this section looks at ways of recruiting applicants with the desired skill and motivation to fill the gaps identified in the employment planning process. The planning process previously described identifies the number and type of employees and *recruitment* seeks to find them. The follow-up stage is to *select* the appropriate personnel. So the recruitment and selection process can be broken down into three stages:

1 Narrow the number of applicants by sifting out those unqualified, insufficiently qualified or those who are not suited to the organisation. (However, those rejected should not feel so rejected that they harbour ill feelings about the firm.)
2 Select the appropriate candidates using appropriate selection techniques.
3 Induct the new personnel to the firm and the work environment.

The process outlined above can be used as the framework to recruiting and selecting staff position or sub-contractors. The difference will be in the techniques applied to each step. Taking each in turn:

1 Extending the pool of applicants for vacancies
The size of the pool of available personnel will be a function of external and internal (to the organisation) factors. Demand for personnel from competitors will expand or shrink the pool of personnel available. This will largely depend upon trading con-

ditions; for example the early to mid 1980s saw an acute manpower crisis hitting the UK construction industry with tradesmen (particularly carpenters and bricklayers), site staff and designers being in short supply especially in the south-east. This was seen as a function of buoyant trading conditions in the south-east leading to a considerable strain on the labour market. Classical economic theory would advocate the adjustment of the wage rates to compensate for shortages and this has been a conventional response. However, recruiters should note that wages are only one factor influencing employment behaviour. Labour economists temper their analysis of naked market forces by suggesting that factors such as location, job security, the job, the fringe benefits, the prospects, etc, have a large influence on behaviour. This agglomeration of factors gives one job a 'net advantage' over another. People look for the maximum 'net advantage' from an employer.

Other external constraints on recruitment may be imposed by client, government or union restrictions. These are probably less influential than the economic position of the industry but in certain instances may play a part in shaping the recruitment pool. The political environment of the late 1970s and 1980s have served to lessen the influence of clients and unions on recruitment strategies. Prior to the Employment Act of 1980 clients (particularly local authorities) could insist on only union members working on their sites. Unions and managements agreed that sub-contractor employees would have to be in union membership. Legislation has removed these options for clients, and the political and legal climate has moved strongly against the type of management/union agreements which were a feature of the 1960s and 1970s. Nonetheless some places of work still retain pre-entry closed shops where union membership is a prerequisite of employment – this is of course a recognition of the custom and practice of employment and can be legally challenged under the terms of the Employment Act 1980.

Not only are there external influences on employment there are internal (organisational) influences. The internal influences will have made recruiters inspect options other than hiring new staff. A common response in the construction industry is to sub-contract work – be it work in the trades, management or technical or design staff for consultants. The advantages and disadvantages of sub-contracting have been fully discussed since the late 1960s and it is not intended to rehearse the argument here. Other responses could be the introduction of paid overtime for staff or redesigning, automating or computerising work to reduce staff requirements, although these latter options would normally only be applicable to head office staff.

Once recruitment has been decided upon then the recruiters will need to identify the job requirements, but this alone may not be sufficient. Different personality types may be required to enhance or complement existing personnel resources. Also the personnel recruited in order to be effective have to match their own personalities with the culture of the firm and its stage of development. For example a house builder/developer will need a different type of project manager to, say, a property development company who may look for someone different from a multi-divisional construction company. The house building firm is operating in a single product market and managers here may be expert in improving efficiency of existing operations rather than looking for new market opportunities for the firm's services. The property developer would typically look for managers who seek market opportunities and regularly take risks. Here the emphasis would be on managing change rather than more efficient performance. The multi-divisional construction company could be said to have many activities, some stable but others changing. Managers in the stable areas can use routine structures and activities whilst managers in the more turbulent areas (say building materials development or computer services to the company) should be looking for new ideas to develop them for the firm.

Sources of personnel

There are two basic sources of personnel – *internal* sources and *external* sources. Where a recruitment drive is directed will be dependent upon many factors, amongst these will be:

1 the state of the labour market – internal recruitment may be the only viable source
2 the level of the job – more junior jobs such as junior site engineers or surveyors have no natural 'internal' source
3 the state of personal development of those in levels below the vacancies
4 the corporate plan – growth, steady state or decline in the particular area
5 expected developments in technology which may change the skills required for the job
6 the maturity of the organisation – a relatively new firm may not have the personnel required for new projects
7 the speed at which the new personnel is required
8 the relative cost of recruiting internally and externally
9 company policy in respect of internal promotions
10 the level of investment in training and development which will influence the capability of the internal resources.

These are some of the factors involved in the decision to recruit internally or externally. Each source will require specific targetting and table 2.4 below lists some familiar avenues for recruiting staff.

Many firms will use a mixture of methods to enhance the effectiveness of recruitment.

Internal		*External*	
1	Notice board/company newspaper	1	Schools careers service
2	Referrals (employees refer friends, relatives to the firm)	2	'Milk round' at colleges and universities
3	Using skills inventories (see page 12)	3	Employment agencies – public and private
		4	Recruitment meetings/fairs/exhibitions
		5	Advertising in newspapers and on radio
		6	Walk-ins (particularly used for unskilled labour and (sometimes sub-contract labour)
		7	Sub-contract gangs

Table 2.4　Sources of personnel

Selection techniques
Obviously the selection technique used will reflect the level of employee sought. Casual callers to the site for operative posts need to be handled differently from staff posts. This section deals with selecting staff for permanent positions within the firm. Several techniques can be used, frequently together. Amongst the techniques reviewed are:

application forms
curriculum vitae
interviews
testing

Application forms
Practically every construction firm uses the application form to select appropriate personnel. The philosophy behind the use of such forms is that previous performance or achievements are a good guide to future behaviour or activity. Therefore data is collected which enables selectors to interpret previous experiences of work, education and interests. However if the best use is to be obtained in using application forms they need to be validated by the record of people in post. For example, if a firm has fifty site managers what are the experiences, education and interests that they disclosed and how do these correlate with their performance? By correlating performance with the biographical data provided then the selector is better placed to predict the successful people. But a note of caution needs to be entered, for an organisation can 'clone' itself,

being staffed by people of identical backgrounds without the infusion of new ideas with consequent long-term stagnation.

Curriculum vitae (cv)

This differs from the application form in that the applicants themselves organise the content and format of the cv. This can reveal the concerns and preoccupations of the candidate. MEGGINSON (1981) identifies the clues to look for in cvs:

- a record of achievement such as upward movement with one employer or horizontal movement between organisations
- responsibility as shown by positions held
- sudden shifts in career movement that may indicate lack of maturity or changed aspirations
- degree of mobility as shown by the number of jobs held compared to years of employment and
- reasons for wanting the job.

Interviews

The use of interviews for job selection is a paradox. It is universally used and (almost) universally derided as a predictor of job success. Research about the validity of interviews has abounded and SCHMITT (1976) in his review found that interviewers frequently overemphasised the importance of negative information given at the interview. Also the interviewers had a very subjective approach to candidate selection with archetypes being sought, those displaying physical or cultural similarity to the interviewer being favoured, or an overemphasis upon visual clues. The factors devalued the use of an interview as an accurate predictive technique.

So why do firms retain the interview as a selection technique? The interview is used to assess the interpersonal qualities so essential for work in construction. Equally all parties expect an interview and therefore it has face validity in that no firm would employ staff without an interview nor would applicants take a job without an interview. So the interview is used for more purposes, such as giving and receiving information as well as making selection decisions.

Testing

There are many proprietary tests available from personnel consultants, frequently a qualified occupational psychologist is necessary to administer them. Tests can be classified on the basis of personal characteristics sought from the candidate. Typically tests can be clustered into four sets which measure:

1 intelligence
2 aptitudes
3 personality
4 achievements.

Intelligence tests
These are not as widely used as they were during the 1960s, because of their proven unreliability but some firms still prefer to administer tests to measure mental or learning ability.

Aptitude tests
These tests measure a person's ability to learn, given the right training, a particular job. Originally developed to predict success in clerical or mechanical jobs they have been shown to reliably predict success in managerial jobs. (GHISELLI 1973.)

Personality tests
These are widely used since 'personality' is seen as a key to success in supervisory and managerial posts in construction. They measure a personality type and this can be correlated with the types already undertaking the jobs successfully. Work by LANGFORD and McDERMOTT (1984) at Brunel University used tests to explore the interpersonal behaviour and prevailing patterns of relationships between members of construction project teams when faced with major variation orders. It was found that where the interpersonal relations, as measured by the test, were good, then variations were dealt with speedily and informally. Where personal relations were not so good or deteriorating, then variations were dealt with formally and more rigidly, leading to delays in expediting the necessary construction work and documentation.

Achievement tests
These tests seek to measure a person's knowledge or proficiency for a particular job. This approach has been widely used in the construction industry for testing the skill level of apprentices. Apprentices are subject to skill tests to measure their proficiency at the trade for which they are being trained.

Inducting new employees
New events are likely to be stressful; none more so than a new job. In construction, site based personnel are faced with new challenges every time they change sites. For the new employee induction procedures will need to focus, in the first instance, upon learning job procedures and company policies. In short, fitting in with the firm's way of doing things. The second objective which may apply to the new starter and persons new to a particular site is to establish relationships with colleagues, be they subordinates or bosses. It is the second element of induction – the social orientation which is the most influential in shaping positive attitudes. The following checklist may be useful in managing the induction of new employees:

1 give basic information first (company policies, procedures, etc)
2 give new employees information about the style and expected standards of their managers, colleagues and subordinates
3 assign an experienced colleague to 'mentor'. This person to provide the necessary detail about the organisation and its procedures
4 gradually widen the circle of contacts within the firm or the site so that the new employee can become 'socialised' into the organisation
5 increase the demands made on a new employee gradually after the contacts and knowledge of procedures are in place.

2.4 Outputs

The conversion process, the tasks undertaken by management, will release the outputs of the sub-system as shown in figure 2.1. The processes undertaken have the objective of ensuring that the manpower sub-system within the company contains the right balance of manpower to achieve the strategic objectives set down by the company.

The outputs of the sub-system when analysed enable the managers of the subsystem (usually the personnel manager) along with other managers to undertake organisational reviews. According to FRYER (1985) 'the purpose (of organisational reviews) is to decide on suitable work structures and formal roles and relationships, to allocate responsibilities, and defence levels of authority'. This information from the outputs can feed back into the overall management system which provided the input to the manpower sub-system.

The outputs will be subject to influences outside the boundaries of the subsystem. Certainly the environment system will influence the social, legal and economic framework and this will shape the inputs to the manpower subsystem. However, within the subsystem the outputs will provide a primary resource for the construction organisation. How conflicts within the organisation are handled, the levels of trust, co-operation and participation which exist can dramatically effect the effectiveness and profitability of the building organisation.

Questions

1 Discuss the implications of the establishment of a specialist personnel department within a building firm.
          CIOB Part II *Building management II* Paper 1 (resit) 1986

2 Recruitment and selection procedures seek to identify the best person for the job by eliminating subjective opinion. Discuss.

CIOB Part II *Building Management II* Paper 1 1986

3 'The average British employer . . . believes that training is not an investment but an overhead . . . is one of those philanthropic things like staff welfare . . . and certainly not something you offer to your established employees.' Mr Brian Nicholson, Chairman of Manpower Services Commission.

Assess this statement in relation to building employers and forecast the likely effect of such an attitude.

CIOB Part II *Building Management II* Paper 1 1987

4 Discuss the objectives of manpower planning to the construction industry and identify the obstacles which may arise when seeking to plan manpower for the individual firm.

3 The Building Materials Sub-system

3.1 Introduction

This chapter considers the Materials Management function in the overall process of construction. Again a systems view is taken and the primary task of the Material Management system is defined as follows:

'To bring to the project the appropriate materials at the right time, quantity and price to enable the construction work to proceed according to programme and to the necessary quality standards.'

The model used for the analysis of the materials management system is shown in figure 3.1. Essentially this system is about materials management and it may be useful to offer a definition. According to the Institute of Materials Handling (1965):

'Materials Management is the name applied to the Management function which co-ordinates and controls these activities in an organisation responsible for the purchasing of materials, their scheduling from supplier and from internal sources, their handling, storage and procurement through the organisation and their delivery to the customers. To assist in this the function must also be responsible for the control of inventory, materials handling, engineering and associated work study and layout planning.'

Clearly the definition defines the materials task on a manufacturing type of operation, and in construction the requirements of a materials management system will need to reflect the uniqueness of the industry. Consequently materials management in construction needs to identify what materials are needed and ensure that they are delivered to site *when* they are needed at a location *where* they are needed. In order to satisfy this requirement certain information is required to enable the process of materials management to be carried out. The information needs have been entitled the *input* to the system and the tasks which follow as the *process* which leads to the *output* as shown in figure 3.1. The boundary of the sub-system is the procurement activity. All environmental factors such as trading conditions, inflation, etc, have not been considered to fall within the sub-system.

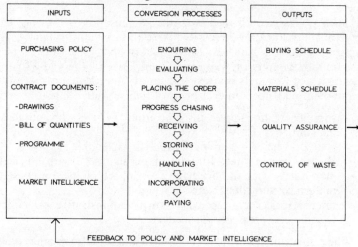

3.1 A systems model for the materials sub-system

The system shown in the diagram begins to be activated when a contractor (or sub-contractor) has been invited to tender for a project. Whilst there has been a move away from traditional contracts over the last ten years much of the physical construction work carried out on sites is based upon competitive tender.

3.2 Inputs

1 The purchasing policy

Binding together the inputs to the Materials Management system will be the purchasing policy. The purchasing policy of a construction organisation will be the body of principles which will guide the buying function of the organisation. Other departments will also have policy; financial policy, and personnel policy are good illustrations. The purchasing policy, as with other departmental policies needs to be integrated with the overall policy of the organisation.

Purchasing policies oversee the conduct of the purchasing function. They will, of necessity, be broad and serve as:

'guidelines to repetititve questions of significance to the organisation and, by the policy statement eliminate misunderstandings and uncertainty. Universally applied they reduce, if not eliminate concern as to discrimination in the minds of suppliers, including tenders. They present a prescribed method to be followed by purchasing personnel and since such policies should be unambiguous they should not allow for variations or differences in approach.'
(FARMER 1985)

Such policies could deal with the organisation of buying, eg, whether sites are allowed to buy materials or whether all materials have to be bought from head office. Alternatively size gates may be set up which limits the purchasing authority of the sites, so for example bags of nails may be bought at site but major pieces of equipment may not. Other aspects of policy could relate to:

- supplier relationships – ensuring ethical behaviour by purchasing staff
- source policies – guiding buyers to particular suppliers, eg British rather than foreign materials; no South African materials; local rather than national suppliers; purchasing materials from clients, etc
- internal policies – these lay down administrative principles which are expressed in procedures.

The policy must, of course, be known and some companies have found it useful to document the policy and the attendant procedures on a purchasing manual. This manual enables the Materials Management system to become a routine operation, not only is such a manual system useful for staff on the buying function but is also useful in pointing up the policies and procedures for potential suppliers. A purchasing manual may typically consist of three sections, organisation, policy and procedures. LYSONS (1981) lays out the contents of a typical purchasing manual thus:

(a) *Organisation*
   (i) Charts showing the place of purchasing within the undertaking and how it is organised both centrally and locally.
   (ii) Job descriptions for all posts within the purchasing function including, where applicable, limitations of authority to commit the undertaking.

(b) *Policy*
   (i) Statements of policy setting out the objectives, responsibilities and authority of the purchasing function.
   (ii) Statements, which can be expanded, of general principle relating to price, quality, etc.
   (iii) Terms and conditions of purchase.
   (vi) Relationships with suppliers especially gifts, entertainment, etc.
   (v) Supplier selection.
   (vi) Employee purchases.
   (vii) Reports to management.

(c) *Procedures*

    (i) Descriptions, accompanied by flow charts, of procedures relating to requisitioning, ordering, expediting, receiving, inspecting, storing and payment for goods.

    (ii) Procedures relating to the rejection and return of goods.

    (iii) Procedures in respect of the disposal of scrap and obsolete or surplus items.

    (iv) Illustrations of all documents used in connection with purchasing and ancillary activities with instructions for their use and circulation.

    (v) Reference to purchase records and their maintenance.

The purchasing manual can set the framework for the activities which make up the materials management system and grade the procedural process described later in this chapter.

Thus the system described can be applicable to large main contractors bidding on a traditional contract or sub-contractors bidding on a management contract or trade contractors looking at trade packages in a construction management contract arrangement.

The parties involved in this system can be the buyer, a materials scheduler, the estimator, the planning engineer and site managers.

2 The contract documents

Here four types of information is considered useful for the Materials Management system:

- the Specification
- the Contract Drawings
- the Bill of Quantities
- Architect's instructions issued during construction.

(a) *The Specification*

At an invitation to tender the Buyer or material scheduler should inspect the specification to identify the materials which have been specified and the tolerances to which these materials have to be incorporated into the construction. The traditional specification gives the constructor information about the standards of construction required and whilst on occasion full descriptions of materials can be given complete with desirable (and undesirable) qualities with the tests the materials will have passed it is more common to merely specify materials which are in accordance with the appropriate British Standard. In all there are six ways in which the buyer can be provided with information about the necessary materials:

1 Full description of the material or component.
2 A relevant British Standard reference.
3 The name of the manufacturer, proprietary brand or source of supply.

4   A brief description of the material with a prime cost for supply
    and delivery of a certain quantity of materials to site.
5   In accordance with National Building Specification (1973). This
    was written as a library of standard specification clauses and
    specification writers combined these clauses to formulate the
    specification. In order to combine clause to exactly meet the
    specific needs the clauses are very short and are coded and
    classified in a way consistent with CI/SB.
6   Performance specification – where the material is specified by
    what it has to do rather than by a description of what material is
    required. This allows considerable flexibility to the materials to
    be purchased but the selected materials will require the approval
    of the designer before incorporation into the structure. To
    support these material specifications the buyer will be provided
    with workmanship clauses. These may tell the buyer much about
    the wastage rate that might be expected from each trade. If
    workmanship tolerances are very tight then the buyer may need
    to consider a greater allowance for waste.

(b)   *The Contract Drawings and Bill of Quantities*
It is likely that the drawings for the project will be a primary source
of information for the buyer and materials scheduler. From the
drawings the materials can be taken off and abstracted to formulate
a materials schedule. Frequently the quantity surveyor will have
undertaken this task and drawings will need to be read in
conjunction with the Bill of Quantities. However, it must be
stressed that quantity in the Bill of Quantities are necessarily
approximate and more accurate scheduling of materials will be
required. Moreover the Bill of Quantities does not indicate the
sequence of work or methods used for construction and these pieces
of information will only be available from the drawing which can
determine what orders need to be placed and when they will be
needed on site. Obviously the construction programme will be a
vital tool in the formulation of the materials schedule.

(c)   *Architect's instruction*
The difficulty with building up materials schedules from drawings
and specifications provided for pre-contract biddings is that they
may change in the course of construction. Architect's instructions
can change the materials used or the quantities of the materials to
be used. Thus the materials schedule needs to be reviewed in the
light of design variations.

3   The programme and method statement

The programme, even if only a pre-tender programme will enable
the buyer to determine when materials are required and the time
when orders have to be placed to enable delivery to be received on

site in a timely fashion. The method statement for particular operations will also provide information about the sequence of activities and this may be crucial in co-ordinating deliveries. The co-ordination of deliveries has become increasingly important in recent times since the re-development of congested inner-city sites coupled with a return to rationalised, partially industrialised, construction methods has meant that many material controllers have scheduled deliveries of (say panels) by the minute to enable the lorry bringing in the material to be turned around in a short period. This 'just-in-time' materials policy has been drawn from the manufacturing industry where minimal stock levels are sought. The approach in construction has been adopted to fit in with constraints imposed by local police authorities who have become increasingly concerned about traffic congestion around construction sites.

4 Market intelligence

One of the major inputs to the materials management process is market intelligence. Knowing where to seek enquiries for materials is of course important but a sensitive intelligence system will also reveal the discounts available on what quantities of order and the quality to be had from the various sources. Much of this information can be found in published journals but this will need to be refined by the buyers local knowledge and experience. The combination of printed material of what is available and native skill comprise the material management market intelligence network. This is vital to successful material management for as specifications move towards 'performance specification' or the flexibility associated with the phrase 'or approved alternative' then the market intelligence function becomes more important. Answers to questions such as: what material is right for the job? where can it be found? what price should we pay for it? when can it be delivered? is the quality reliable?, etc, become vital components fo the materials management system.

3.3 The processes

1 Materials management process

The product of the inputs will be a *materials schedule* and this document will largely direct the user through the somewhat mechanistic process of managing the materials element of construction production. Put simply the process follows the chain shown in figure 3.2.

(a) *The enquiry stage*

The first step in the process will be to use the materials schedule to build up a requisition list – a list of what materials are required. This

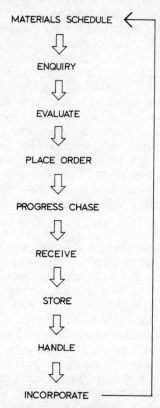

3.2   A materials management process

will then feed the enquiry stage which involves sending out
invitations to suppliers to price the materials needed. The quotation
received at the tender stage may be adequate but they may need to
be adjusted in line with any revised programme. Equally communication between the site, the buyer and the supplier is important.
Issues such as packaging and handling of the materials off of lorries
may be vital. Deliveries to congested inner city sites may be
restricted to nights or weekends.

   After such checks have been made the order can be placed. This
is usually done on a purchase order form. This will include details
such as:

   – suppliers name and address
   – description and quantity of supply
   – any necessary quality assurance certificates required
   – specification and workmanship standard references
   – cross references to any relevant drawings
   – the agreed price plus any discounts or rebates

- time when goods required
- retentions
- liquidated damages
- responsibility for loss or damage of the materials.

The evaluation stage is difficult for it involves reducing competing quotes to a common base so that they may be compared. It should be noted that the invitation to quote for the contractor constitutes a legal offer and the suppliers quote based upon his terms and conditions constitute a 'counter offer' not an acceptance of the original offer. Before any order is placed the two different terms and conditions may need to be reconciled.

(b) *The evaluation stage*
After receiving the quotes they will need to be evaluated. The evaluation will need to take into account the following:

- Basic price
- Discounts
- Surcharges
- Delivery time
- Location of supplier
- Part-load price
- Quality of product including quality assurance requirements
- Payment structure
- Transit charges
- Disputes procedure if quality standards are challenged
- Where the goods are required
- The full set of terms and conditions under which the order is placed.

This order acts as the instrument for getting materials to the site.

(c) *Placing the order*
After the evaluation we are in a position to place the order provided that the contract has been awarded. The buyer will need to select those suppliers who will be invited to tender and how the business is to be placed. Terms and conditions of purchase must be defined at this stage with all potential suppliers to be asked to quote on identical terms.

Delivery dates expected must obviously be specified and when the quote is expected.

(d) *Progress chasing*
In order to ensure that the materials are delivered to site the materials must be expedited at the right time. The progress chasing of materials is frequently the role of the site manager or his assigned nominee. The difficulty with this approach has been identified by

ILLINGWORTH and THAIN (1987) who note that 'this (progress chasing) can be time consuming; other activities may be given priority . . . and the majority of sites may be neglected'. The alternative to progress chasing from site is to undertake the work from head office but good communication between site and head office is essential. Particular attention should be paid to non-standard items where detailed drawings of the component have to be produced by the supplier and approved by the principal designer.

The process of scheduling and progress chasing materials has been made easier by the introduction of a computer package which processes information about lead items for materials delivery and links this information with the construction network. The linking of the two programmes enables the dates for placing and expediting orders to be tracked easily. Early and late order dates for different materials can be identified.

(e) Receiving the materials

The materials need to be checked for quantity and quality upon delivery to site. Quantity inspection is easily done if materials are delivered in bundled units but measuring rods to check timber lengths or reinforcement are useful devices.

With respect to quality checks several stages may be useful to verify the quality of what is delivered. Visual inspections are the lowest level plus tests to see if the delivery complies with the specification or with the appropriate British Standards.

It is easier to reject materials at this stage than wait until the materials are in place on the structure.

Finally, the equipment available for offloading the materials must be compatible with the materials themselves.

(f) Storing the materials

It has long been known that a primary source of waste of building materials is improper storage. Correct storage can also assist in the production process by the correct location of materials so to avoid unnecessary double handling. When considering storage of materials several factors need to be taken into account:

- material lock-ups for expensive and portable materials.
- protection of materials which can deteriorate if exposed to the elements eg cement, plaster, plaster board
- access for any necessary mechanical equipment needed to handle materials
- location of materials as close as practical to their intended use
- the use and location of any off-site storage dumps
- location of materials close to any other complementary materials (eg sand, aggregate)

- safety in the storage of bulk materials so that they cannot fall on workers or passers-by
- adequate arrangements for the receipt and storage of sub-contractors materials.

(g) *Handling and incorporating the materials*

Appropriate handling materials needs to be considered in the materials management process. Moving the materials from site to position of fixing can prove difficult particularly in congested sites. However, the use of fork lift trucks allied to palletised materials has assisted the movement of materials around site. Equally the philosophy of prefabrication with instantaneous incorporation of the materials into the structure can improve construction performance. Steel frames and cladding panels, even complete toilet units can be so incorporated without a need to store materials on site. However, the appropriate handling equipment must be available to enable such rapid construction techniques to take place.

(h) *Paying for the materials*

At some time after receiving the materials and signing for the receipt the suppliers will want paying. The *Goods Received* note made out on site will indicate what and how much material has been received. This is then passed on to the buyers at Head Office. This is then checked against the invoice received from the supplier. An important control function for the materials management system is to ensure that the accounts department do not pay for anything other than approved materials. Provided that the purchaser is satisfied, then payment is made against the invoice. Obviously the payments made will need to be reconciled with the materials schedules to ensure that the materials losses are in line with expectations.

3.4 Outputs

It has been stressed that the Materials Management system has the ultimate objective of facilitating construction production. The materials process outlined earlier is largely mechanistic but produces two essential documents used on the Materials Management system. They are:

1   the buying schedule
2   the materials schedule.

In addition Materials Management will need to consider:

(a)   Quality Assurance and
(b)   the control of waste.

1 The buying schedule

This document will be produced from the enquiry stage of the materials process. Essentially it will record the following information:

- Who is to provide the various types of materials to the project?
- What is to be provided by the supplier?
- When is it to be provided?
- Where is it to be supplied?
- Who is the person responsible at the suppliers end?

The correct information to these questions can make a substantial impact upon a construction organisation in two important ways:

(a) By continuous market research in preparation of the buying schedule and skilful negotiation the buyer can reduce prices paid for materials.
(b) By involvement in the materials industry the buying schedule can identify reliable suppliers.

Such actions can have an impact upon the cost of construction production, directly by the cost of materials incorporated into the structure and indirectly by ensuring that the supply of materials does not stifle constructive production by late or poor quality materials.

The buying schedule will reflect the patterns of market movements in materials and may need to anticipate shortages or gluts of various materials and structure the purchases accordingly. For example if a shortage of a particular material is envisaged then the buying schedule should acknowledge this by spreading an order across several suppliers so that risks of delivery are spread. Conversely gluts can enable a different negotiating strategy for prices to take place.

The buying schedule should also recognise that the market for construction materials is an international one and the suppliers listing should reflect this.

2 The materials schedule

The Materials Schedule is then developed from the buying schedule and the results of the materials take off undertaken during the materials management process. It will provide the detailed information which will enable the materials to be controlled to ensure that construction can take place. Whilst the buyers schedule is used to identify the major issues such as the four Ws, *Who*, *What*, *When* and *Where* the Materials Schedule amplifies this and can be used to provide the following information:

- those materials which will be provided by the sub-contractors

- those materials with long lead time or requiring other special attention
- whereabouts on the site the materials are to be delivered (gate numbers, etc)
- an aide-memoire for expediting deliveries
- a record of the materials which have been delivered and consequently a status report on materials
- an enabling document for materials reconciliation.

3 Quality Assurance procedures

An important product of the Materials Management system is the installation of Quality Assurance procedures for the materials to be incorporated into the structure. Quality assurance is a procedure by which the design process, the manufacture of construction materials and installation meet the clients quality standards; but not only must the standards be achieved but the processes used to achieve the desired quality must be documented. Thus the Materials Management system must ensure that the materials supplied comply not only with the specification but come complete with a quality assurance certification. The materials are then seen to match quality assured standards.

4 Waste control

The final output of the Materials Management system is the control of waste. The cost of materials and handling up to the point of fixing constitutes about 50% of the value of a traditional building contract. The BRE (1982) identified five principles in limiting waste on site. They were:

- pre-plan stacking and storage areas related to site layout
- checking vehicles and materials on arrival
- accounting for materials including recording waste levels
- employment of materials advisor
- use of Schedule of Materials.

The digest then goes on to detail the causes of waste which may be experienced at different stages of the project including the pre-construction stage, the offloading, storage, during incorporation of the materials and the protection of the work after completion.

Earlier work from the BRE by SKOYLES (1982) identified two basic types of wastage *direct waste* and *indirect waste*. SKOYLES (op cit) decribed direct waste as occurring when materials were damaged or lost during construction. The account for this type of loss was seen as a simple accounting procedure which materials reconciliation would pick up. The indirect waste was distinguished from direct waste because it did not represent a waste of materials but could be expressed as a monetary loss. The paper sub-divided indirect waste into 3 classifications; substitution waste, production waste and negligence waste.

(a) *Substitution waste*
This occurs where higher grade materials are used, eg placing high strength concrete in place of weak-mix or facing bricks replacing commons, wrot softwood in place of sawn timber, etc.
   Often the substitution is deliberate in that the small quantities of a substituted material makes it uneconomical to place a separate order.

(b) *Production waste*
This is often unavoidable due to the dictates of the construction process, eg the foundations may not be the width of an excavator bucket and therefore they have to be overdug – here good design may reduce wastage.

(c) *Negligence waste*
This arises from errors, eg poor work condemned, setting out errors, overdug excavations etc. It is difficult to ascribe this directly to waste but it must be accounted for somewhere.

The control of waste can be built into the Materials Management system by site management undertaken 'Anti-Wastage' campaigns or by the appointment of a Materials Advisor. The duty of this person would be to investigate materials losses and to check materials requisitions against the allowances made in the Materials Schedule. This task then leads to materials reconciliation which can monitor the use of materials and isolate areas of proligacy. If production efficiency is the desired objective then an appropriate Materials Management system must be incorporated into the project and Corporate Management system.

Questions

1 The responsibility for the purchase of building materials may be vested in site management or in its central buying department. Present arguments for and against the use of each method.
   CIOB Part I *Building Management I* 1986

2 Detail an organisation structure and associated set of procedures likely to ensure efficient and effective materials management in building contracting.
   CIOB Part II *Building Management II* Paper 1 1987

3 Materials control has become a central feature of a building organisation's operations. Analyse the forces which have led to an increasing concern to control materials and discuss how building organisations may seek to ensure the desired control over materials acquisition and utilisation.

4 (a) Where no working space exists outside the building area on a congested city site suggest ways and means of overcoming, in an economical fashion the problems related to:

    (i) materials delivery

    (ii) materials storage.

  (b) Outline the precautions to be taken on a building site to minimise the wastage and loss of materials.

4 The Construction Plant Sub-System

4.1 Introduction

This chapter again uses the systems approach to analyse the use of construction plant in building organisations. Again inputs; the processes required to convert these inputs into an output; and the output of the system itself are discussed.

We can see in figure 4.1 the model which is used for the analysis of this chapter. It will be seen that the inputs are a mixture of policies of the organisation, the construction methods used on a project and the skills of the plant managers themselves. The processes used to convert this construction plant into the output again uses a flow model similar to that used in chapter 9. The primary task of the plant management sub-system is 'to bring to the project that construction plant which can enable construction work to proceed according to programme and serve the site labour in an appropriate manner'. This statement is of itself a recognition that few countries in the world are able to build as fast as they would like and construction plant is required to enhance construction productivity. Indeed debate in the latter part of the 1980s has focussed upon the need for construction methods and contractual systems which are able to deliver buildings to the client faster than before. Clearly plant has a vital role to play in the realisation of such objectives.

The boundary of the sub-system is the plant and equipment activity. Related systems such as strategic, financial, production and management sub-systems will influence the behaviour of the plant sub-system but are ignored for purposes of this discussion.

Developments in mechanisation and construction plant have played an increasingly important part in improving productivity. The need for construction plant has equally been emphasised by the critical labour shortages which periodically beset the construction industry. No longer do we have vast numbers of skilled men and women available for crash building programmes. Indeed, even if such a reserve army of labour were available then the economics of construction would prohibit their use. Therefore, increasingly the construction industry has looked towards using plant and machinery to speed up the construction process, but for successful performance during construction the opportunities for mechanisation should be taken at the design stage. This imposes new demands on the designer; not only does the creative process have to be

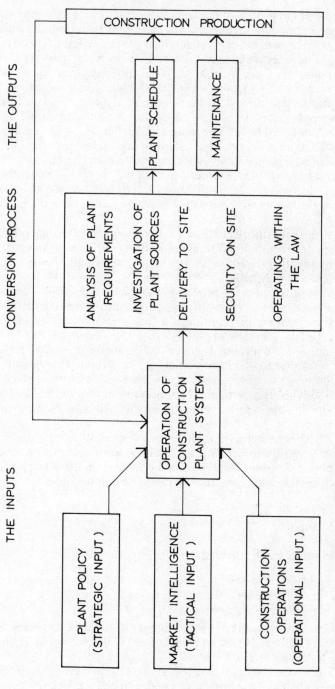

4.1 *The plant management sub-system*

satisfied but aspects of the knowledge and techniques of production engineering need to be incorporated into the design in order to obtain the benefits of mechanisation at the site level. This is not to say that mechanisation in construction is an easy task. The conditions of production are very different from those which pertain in the factory where production methods ensure that materials are moved to the machine. By contrast, construction materials have to be assembled in situ and consequently the machines used have to be more mobile. Further, each site is a new installation; it operates for a short period and no process is carried out at a single location – concreting, brick-laying, etc, are carried out at many places around a building site, consequently the mechanisation of such operations is difficult. The work cannot be brought to the machine so the machine has to be brought to the work.

A further difficulty in the mechanisation of the building process is that construction operations are seldom continuous. An operation is frequently phased and consequently the actual utilisation of the machinery may be low.

One of the primary problems in the mechanisation of construction work is the divorcing of design and construction and this may be a major factor in retarding the progress of mechanisation. A contractor is usually appointed after the design has either been completed or conceptualised, and therefore the contractor has little opportunity to exert an influence on production methods in traditional contracts. And yet, as has been seen, the production methods selected influence the opportunities for mechanisation.

Finally, the weather impedes progress to a more mechanised industry.

All of these factors make it impossible to apply as high a degree of mechanisation to construction which is associated with a modern factory operation. Nevertheless mechanisation has a large part to play in increasing construction production in building.

4.2 Inputs

The inputs can be divided into three types. They are:

1 the strategic inputs
2 the tactical input; and
3 the operational input.

The strategic issue feeding the system will be the plant policy. Such a policy will need to reflect plant holding policies and relating this to the tendering strategy.

The tactical issues will relate to market intelligence of the plant department and the programme and methods used in construction.

The operational aspects relate to the construction techniques used on site and whilst these may be determined by the design, the contractor has some flexibility in the choice of plant to be used. These then constitute the inputs and will be converted to outputs by the processes carried out by the plant department. Amongst these conversion processes will be the analysis of plant requirements, investigation of plant resources and an assessment of the duration of requirements. If these processes are carried out correctly then they should ensure that plant works effectively and is well maintained to ensure that construction production is maintained.

The arrangement for the sub-system is shown in figure 4.1. Considering each element of the inputs in turn.

1 Plant policy

As with any other departmental policy the plant and equipment policy needs to fit in to the overall company policy. As we have seen the company policy will address broad strategic issues which shape the company and its direction. Questions such as 'what kind of contract will the firm bid for?' and 'what kind of procurement methods are seen as advantageous for the company?' For example, a company who are dedicated to heavy civil engineering work and can see themselves as specialists in this area of the construction market, will obviously need a very different plant holding policy to firms which, for example, undertake large contracts but only on the basis of a fee or management contract. In the latter situation the plant will be held or hired by the trade contractors or sub-contractors and that the management contractor will merely have to provide the necessary site services. Equally, the plant holding position for a smaller contractor dedicated to maintenance and refurbishment work will need to reflect the nature of the work and is therefore likely to have a greater proportion of hand held equipment than a larger civil engineering firm.

A second issue will be the spread of activity for a contractor. A firm with a wide portfolio will want to have a plant policy which reflects the breadth of activity and therefore more generalised type of equipment may be held. A specialised firm on the other hand may have a focussed policy holding the particular specialist equipment and hiring in more general needs. For many contractors the strategic issue is maintaining flexibility rather than exercising cost reduction as a goal. Consequently the holding of plant for non-general use is restricted (WINCH 1985). Thirdly, the methods used in construction will shape the policy. If a firm is able to standardise the methods then this may direct the plant policy, but as we have seen, methods are frequently dependent upon designs and in a traditional setting, contractors have limited influence upon these.

Another major area of policy is in the area of charges levied on the site from the plant department here. Several options exist: 1

internal plant charges may reflect the general state of the plant hire market and the sites pay the going rate. Alternatively, notional or nominal charges may be made which reflect the marginal costs of holding the plant and not the full costs. Again this will be a policy decision which the company needs to make.

The third arena for policy is the relationship between the plant department and the site. Often the site will wish to have autonomy in selecting a particular piece of equipment for a particular job, even if the plant department has an equivalent machine in the plant yard. The process of formulating policy will need to address the duties and responsibilities and the limitations of authority of site in respect of plant.

Finally, the plant policy may wish to address the duties and responsibility of the sites in respect of maintenance. Here there may be conflicting demands; time spent on maintenance whilst the plant is at site may be regarded as downtime by site management. On the other hand the plant yard managers may regard maintenance as essential function which has to be carried out during the course of site operations, not just when the plant is in the yard.

To sum up, plant policy must serve as guidelines for the conduct of the plant management function. They will of necessity be broad and seek to direct the conduct of the department and its relationships with the sites.

2   Market intelligence

One of the major functions of a plant department will be to provide market intelligence to the top management regarding new pieces of equipment and an overall plant strategy. Secondly, to provide the estimating department with anticipated outputs from various types of machinery and thirdly, to provide the sites with an intelligence system which identifies the correct piece of equipment for the particular needs of the site.

Considering firstly the role of the plant department in relation to senior management, here issues such as the amount of investment in plant and machinery need to be addressed along with the analysis of the best mix of owned and hired plant. Moreover, the sources of the plant to be owned along with the relative capital costs and any source of financial support for such capital investments. These may be tax allowances or grant aid from government or local government programmes. The current position is that capital payments do not attract tax benefit and in this situation the plant policy may be to buy cheaper second-hand plant and maintain it at will. This option is attractive as maintenance costs can be set against earnings before tax. A further issue for the plant department to advise top management is the provision for and structure of a maintenance organisation. Policy options are open here so that certain construction organisations may have their own in-house facilities or arrange for servicing to be undertaken on a contract basis. A plant department will also have to offer market intelligence to the estimators. Consideration to plant requirements for the degree of mechanisation to be applied to a particular contract should start at an early stage in the pre-tender programme. Machines will have an important effect upon the size of the labour force to be used on a particular project and the balance of the labour force. However, a note of caution needs to be made. The more that machines are used the more dependent we become on them for increased productivity and the more serious are the consequences of a breakdown. The breakdown of a hoist, a crane, and a mixer can bring a site to a halt. Therefore selecting the appropriate plant is an important market intelligence function. Apart from plant manufacturers' advertisements in articles in the technical press, a good way of keeping abreast of plant developments is to go to the international exhibitions, or to attend manufacturers' demonstrations, provided of course that these are staged realistically. Previous experience will obviously be a primary source of intelligence to be provided to the estimators. Analytical techniques such as work study, etc, can be most useful in evaluating the effectiveness of various pieces of plant.

3 Construction operations

The process of managing the plant fleet cannot be divorced from the planning and technical aspects of construction operations. A contractor offering particular technical expertise in one area of construction technology will need to have the plant and to manage the plant in particular ways. For example road building specialists will have to have different plant from contractors primarily involved in property development. However this stark contrast has other implications in that the firm involved in property development is more likely to be driven by time, rather than cost considerations and the design is likely to reflect a necessity for speedy completion with a high level of plant utilisation assumed because of the necessity to maintain rapid levels of production. In contrast the civil engineering road builder may have an equally large, albeit different, plant holding but uses it to undertake work which is by tradition highly mechanised, eg earth moving. The design of such projects is not likely to be too sensitive to time savings and cost reduction is more likely to be the primary objective. In both cases the construction operations are shaping the plant tactics of the contractor. Therefore the operations themselves are providing an input to the plant management process.

Equally the construction planning at the pre-tender stage will assist in shaping the selection of the appropriate plant for each type of job. The clients expectation of when the project is to be completed will shape the perception of plant use by construction and these pressures can do much to inject thinking about the mechanisation of construction process by the design team and the contractors.

4.3 The conversion processes

The inputs to the plant sub-system lead to certain processes which enable the plant to be managed effectively. These processes can be presented as a flow chart of activities which result in a *plant* schedule which is a key document to control plant on site. The flow chart is shown below:

The processes
Analysis of plant requirements (type and duration)
Investigation of the sources of the plant
Delivery to site
Security on site
Operating the plant within the legal framework.

1   Analysis of plant requirements
This process can be broken down into two aspects:

(a)   type of plant required;
(b)   duration of the plant requirement.

The origin of such decisions need to be considered in the pre-tender planning stage for it is here that the opportunities for mechanisation will present themselves. Moreover, how the pre-tender planning team address the issue of mechanisation will be reflected in the tender price. The methods of construction envisaged will also influence the type of plant used whilst the pre-tender programme will influence its duration on site. Consequently the analysis of plant requirements needs to be developed from pre-tender documents such as the method statement and the pre-tender programme. Such documents can enable reviews of the prospective methods and durations and can allow alternatives to be developed so that comparisons between method and types of plant can be made. The pre-tender programme and method statement can be used to yield information about the duration on site of particular pieces of plant and the expected performance of the plant in the particular site conditions. This can lead to an estimate of the numbers of pieces of plant and the labour required to operate and service the plant. This information can guide the plant department and pre-tender programmers to decisions about the sources of the plant.

One of the important pre-tender decisions about the type of plant will be the amount of noise and other environmental pollution that the plant may create.

The Control of Pollution Act (1974) charges local authorities with the control of noise from building sites. The permissible noise will vary with the type and location of the works. If the plant to be used on site is likely to create very noisy conditions the contractor can ask the local authority to make its requirements known which results in a 'consent' certificate which specifies the acceptable noise levels. Plant can then be matched with this requirement. Most plant manufacturers have noise reduced versions of standard equipment.

It is worth noting that the contractor does not have to apply to a local authority for a 'consent' but not doing so runs the risk of being served with one after the site works have started. This can be wasteful and disruptive.

2 Investigation of plant sources

As has been mentioned there are several potential sources of plant for a site. To recap, they are:

- from the firms own plant holding
- purchasing new plant for the job
- specialist plant hire firms
- leasing arrangements.

Which of these sources is most appropriate will depend upon a multitude of factors. MEAD and MITCHELL (1972) have identified six major factors which influence decisions concerning the source of plant. They are:

(a) Economics
(b) Type and condition of the company's own plant fleet
(c) Type of project
(d) The duration of the plant requirement
(e) The availability of operators
(f) The location of the site in relation to the plant depot.

Considering each in turn:

(a) *Economics*
The pre-tender plan may have revealed that the project requirements exceed the capacity of the plant depot. This then presages a decision to buy in more plant or to hire or lease the balance. If the plant is of a general nature and is likely to find application on a number of sites then it may be desirable to buy in, but if the plant is specialised then hiring may be a more prudent source of action.

Short term hire of specialist equipment is more likely to be more economic but the decision whether to lease, on a long term or buy a piece of plant is more marginal.

The economic comparisons will need to be made but these should guide not rule decisions and other factors related to the purchasing capacity of the company as a whole to be taken into account. A capital outlay may be more difficult to find as opposed to smaller amounts paid regularly to the leaser. Assumptions about the life expectancy of the plant will also be a vital component in the calculation. However, by making some assumptions we can compare the two methods.

Assuming a four year life for a piece of plant and an interest rate of 10% on money borrowed. The plant costs £20,000 and may be leased at £4000 over six months.

Year	Half year	Period	Purchase	Lease
0			−20,000	
	1	1		−4,000
	2	2		−4,000
1				
	1	3		−4,000
	2	4		−4,000
2				
	1	5		−4,000
	2	6		−4,000
3				
	1	7		−4,000
	2	8		−4,000
4				

Now these figures have to be put into present worth setting. This technique enables the value of the £20,000 investment in terms of its present day value. The present worth of the leasing arrangement is calculated by applying the following formula. It may then be compared to the purchase price

$$\frac{(1 + i)^n - 1}{i (1 + i)^n}$$

Where i is the interest rate and
n is the number of periods considered.

Firstly we need to find the half year interest rate assuming an annual rate of 10%

$(I + i_{\text{half year}})^2 = (I + i_{\text{year}})$
$**(I + _{\text{half year}})^4 = (I \cdot 10)^1$
$**i_{\text{half year}} = 2\sqrt{(I \cdot I)} - I = 0 \cdot 048 = 4 \cdot 8$

Using the present worth formula we obtain the following present worth figures:

$$(I + 0.048)^8 - I = \frac{0.455}{0.0628} = 6.518.$$
$$0.048 (I + 0.048)^8$$

Monthly leasing costs £4,000 × 6·518 = £26,072
Purchase cost   £20,000

On the evidence the purchase cost of £20,000 is more attractive than the net present value of the lease costs.

However, this comparison does not take into account inflation or any tax relief associated with capital investment in plant.

If tax is payable at 50% then £10,000 can be saved from the company tax bill. This is 'saved' in the year following the purchase of the plant and therefore has to be presented as a net present value.

Year	Purchase	Tax Saving	Present worth at 10%interest (from tables)	Present worth
0	−20,000		1.0	−20000
1		+10,000	0.909	+ 9090
				−£10910

So the real cost of buying is £10910. However the cost of leasing also has tax relief for it is a trading expense and can be deducted from revenue before tax (HARRIS and MCCAFFER 1982).

So after one year the amount paid in the previous year leasing the plant can be set against tax. So:

Year	Period	Leave	Tax reduction	Net present value	Present worth of tax reduction
1	1	4000			
	2	4000			
2	3	4000		0.8264	
	4	4000	2000		1652.80
3	5	4000			
	6	4000	2000	0.7513	1502.60
4	7	4000			
	8	4000	2000	0.6830	1366
5			2000	0.6209	1241.8
					5762.2

So the actual cost of leasing over the period is

$$£26360 - £5763.20 = £20596.$$

In the given circumstances the buy option looks more attractive but these figures will change as the interest rate, the duration of deferment of tax relief and the life of the plant change.

(b)   Type and quality of the company's plant

A part of the plant policy discussed earlier would have likely to have been that plant held in the plant yard must be used prior to sites entering into hire agreements. However, in order to ensure that this policy does not create dissatisfaction at the project level, then the plant supplied to sites must be of an appropriate type and be sufficiently well maintained to ensure that it can operate reliably for the duration of the requirement.

For sites with large plant needs this may necessitate a site based maintenance servicing operation.

(c)   Type of project

The plant stock held by contractors will need to reflect the type of work which the contractor seeks. For some firms the strategic task will be to specialise and consequently become market leaders in a niche within the overall market. This strategy would dictate a narrow range of plant holding with a high degree of specialisation. However, for most firms within the industry the strategic objective is to retain flexibility to be able to tender and service a wide range of construction activity. Frequently the organisation structure reflects specialisms through the creation of departments, eg the small works department, special projects division, management contracting division, etc, and these specialised groupings frequently share common services such as staff and particularly plant and equipment. Thus the corporate objective is to retain flexibility in the face of volatile market conditions and this itself will direct the plant holding policy – general as opposed to specialist plant being necessary in most cases.

(d)   Duration of the plant requirement

How long a piece of plant is required on site will be dependent on the task and the quantity of work involved. These factors will, in turn, influence the appropriate source of the plant. For example, most sites have a dumper truck available for the duration of the works so that fetching and carrying can be done – this type of requirement may be best serviced from the firms own fleet for the requirement is long enough to warrant the holding of such plant. In contrast a concrete pump or mobile crane may only be required intermittently and consequently best hired in. The principle is that sporadic needs are best served by plant hire arrangements. This may apply to the type of plant or the numerical requirement of more commonplace items.

(e)   The availability of operators

Many pieces of plant require certificated operators, eg tower cranes, lorry drivers, large earthmoving equipment; many more require trained and experienced operators to obtain the most effective utilisation of the plant. Consequently when considering the sources of plant for a project the availability of operators needs to be taken into account. With increased complexity of plant it is vital that operator training is taken seriously.

(f)   Location

The location of the site to be serviced with plant may influence the decision about the sources of plant. If the site is very distant from the plant yard, then the costs of transporting equipment from the yard to the site may mean that hiring plant from sources close to the site is more economical. Whilst mathematical models are available to determine whether it is cheaper to hire locally or transport plant to the site, they are seldom used in practice. As usual management judgement is the key skill required in making such decisions.

3   Delivery to site

This is a fairly procedural issue and merits little discussion. However, the plant yard should check the following points when arranging delivery of plant to sites:

- is the plant to travel under its own power or be transported by lorry or low loader? (If the plant is to travel on a public highway then the driver must have an 'operator's licence')
- does the plant require any police permits either in travelling certain routes or in blocking traffic when it is being unloaded or assembled at site? (Tower cranes and other large equipment for inner city sites can cause particular traffic difficulties)
- is any special routing necessary to avoid particular obstacles, eg low bridges or load restricted bridges, etc?
- is any particular access arrangement necessary? Eg will an excavating machine have to cross private land to gain access to the site, if so what arrangements have to be made with the landowner
- Is any ancillary equipment for unloading the plant at the site necessary?
- Is any specialist labour required to assist in the delivery process? eg fitters to help offload and assemble.

4 Security on site

Security may be interpreted in two ways:

Firstly the prevention of theft, an increasingly common problem, and secondly the safety of the site personnel and casual, but not malicious, intruders. Some guidelines on these aspects are given.

Freedom from theft
- Use a lock up store for hand held equipment, eg power saws, repercussive hammers, etc
- where necessary use a compound for items of large plant; where this is not possible immobilise the plant overnight and at weekends
- Sophisticated security systems are available to mark plant and assist in the retrieval of stolen equipment, for example the Cousec system.

Safety of the site environs
- Do not park plant on slopes
- Eliminate, as far as possible access to the plant. Children tend to find construction plant attractive for play
- The use of Watchmen who are alert to the danger associated with plant on site.

5 The legal framework for plant management

Finally the process involved in plant management will need to ensure that the plant is operated and maintained within the framework of the law governing the operation of plant. This need for compliance has implications beyond mere observation of the law – the safety of employees, sub-contractors and visitors to site is at issue. Regularly construction workers are killed by construction equipment and typically accidents involving transport and machinery constitute 20% of the fatal accidents each year. The Health and Safety Executive (1988) produced a report, (Transport) kills which highlighted the hazards associated with site plant. Of the eighty fatal accidents involving transport during the period 1978–80 some sixty-one of the deaths were caused by earth moving equipment or transport vehicles. Another disturbing feature of the report was that 30% of the accidents were attributed to inadequate training of plant operators.

The principal piece of legislation governing the use of plant and equipment is the Health and Safety at Work Act 1974. This Act provided a comprehensive framework for the governance of health and safety at the place of work. The Act itself is of necessity general but is supported by specific regulations which give detailed guidance on safe provision of plant. Particular Regulations are listed below:

Factory Acts 1961
Construction (General Provisions) Regulations 1961
Construction (Lifting Operations) Regulations 1961.

Obviously there are many more sets of regulations which pertain to the construction industry but the ones listed above are most relevant to plant operators. Particular care should be taken when statutory tests, examinations and inspections are required. These are summarised in a list prepared by George Wimpey and appeared in *Building Technology and Management* in March 1974, and was reprinted in *Construction Plant* by HARRIS and McCAFFER (1982).

4.4 Outputs

The principal product of these considerations in the pre-contract stage will be a plant schedule. This will be a programme which identifies the type of plant and when it will be required on a bar chart. Supporting this could be details of ancillary equipment, maintenance needs and the operators necessary to work the plant. A typical plant schedule is shown in figure 4.2.

This document is then used to control the use of plant on the site and will ensure that the plant provided matches the production requirements of the site. It is by managing the plant function that productivity within the industry can be improved. Plant has a vital part to play in the elusive yet most necessary outcome.

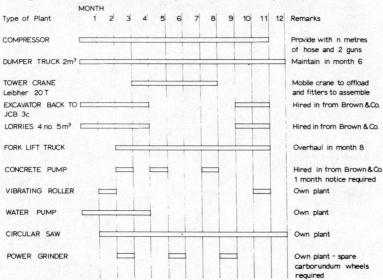

4.2   A typical plant schedule

Construction Operations

| Type of plant equipment or job involved | A Testing and thorough examination | | | B Thorough |
	Testing and thorough examination	Who carries out this work	Results to be recorded on Form No	Thorough examination
Scaffolding				
Excavations **Earthworks** **Trenches** **Shafts and Tunnels**				Weekly or more often if part has been affected, eg explosives collapse
Materials or timber used to construct or support trenches **excavations,** **coffer dams** **caissons**				
Coffer dams **caissons**				Before men are employed therein and at least weekly or more often if explosives are used or any part damaged
Dangerous atmospheres				Before men are employed therein and as frequently as necessary
Cranes (all types) **Crabs** **Winches**	Once every four years and after substantial alteration or repair	Competent person, normally by insurance co. engineer, manu-facturer or erector	Crane: form 96 Crab: form 80 Winch: form 80	At least every 14 months
Pulley blocks **Gin wheels** **Sheer legs**	Before first use and after alteration or substantial repair unless used only for loads under 1 ton	Competent person, normally the manu-facturer or insurance company engineer	Form 80	At least every 14 months
Cranes appliances for anchorage or ballasting				On each occasion before crane is erected
Cranes test of anchorage or ballasting	Before crane is taken into use, ie after each erection or re-erection on a site or whenever anchorage or ballasting arrang. changed	Competent person, normally crane erector in presence of insurance company engineer	Form 91 (pt I) D	Has to be done after exposure of crane to weather conditions likely to have affected its stability. A re-test might be necessary

examination		C Inspection			D References
Who carries out this work	*Results to be recorded on Form No*	*Inspection to be carried out*	*Who carries out this work*	*Results to be recorded on Form No*	*Legal reference*
		Weekly or more often in bad weather	Competent person	Form 91 (pt 1) A	WP regn 22
Competent person	Form 91 (pt 1) B entry to be made day of examination	At least every day or at start of shift	Competent person		GP regn 9
		On each occasion before use	Competent person	GP regn 10 (1) GP regn 17 (2)	
Competent person	Form 91 (pt 1) B	Daily and before men are employed therein	Competent person		GP regn 18
Competent person Instrument may be necessary	In any convenient way to show how examination was done				GP regn (21)(c)
Competent person eg insurance company engineer	Form 91 (pt II) J or on a special filing card containing the prescribed particulars	Weekly	Competent person e.g. crane driver	Form 91 (pt I) C-F	LO regn 10 (1) (c) LO regn 28 (1) (2) and (3)
Competent person, eg insurance company engineer	Form 91 (pt II) J or on special filing card containing the prescribed particulars	Weekly	Competent person	Form 91 (pt I) C-F	LO regn 10 (1) (2) LO regn 28 (1) and (2)
Competent person, eg crane erector or fitter					LO regn 19 (3)
Competent person, eg insurance company					LO regn 19 (4)

Continued. . .

A Testing and thorough examination B Thorough

Type of plant equipment or job involved	Testing and thorough examination	Who carries out this work	Results to be recorded on Form No	Thorough examination
Cranes test of automatic safe load indicator (jib cranes)	After erection or installation of crane and before it is taken into use	Crane erector or insurance company engineer; must be a competent person with knowledge of the working arrangements of indicator	Form 91 (pt I) E	
Cranes mobile jib test of automatic safe load indicator	Before crane is taken into use, after it has been dismantled or after anything has been done which is likely to affect the proper operation of indicator, eg change in jib length	Competent person, eg erector, manufacturer, engineer, insurance company	Form 91 (pt I)	
Lifting other **appliances** ie excavator dragline piling frame, aerial cableway or ropeway, overhead runway				At least every 14 months or after substantial alteration or repair
Hoists (goods) made altered or repaired after 1 March 1962	Before first use and after substantial alteration or repair	Competent person, manufacturer or insurance company engineer	Form 75	At least every 6 months
Hoists passenger	Before first use, after re-erection, alterations in height of travel after repair or alterations	Competent person, eg manufacturer, insurance company engineer or erector	Form 75 or form 91 (pt I) F following alterations to height of travel	At least every 6 months
Chains rope slings and lifting gear	Before first use and after alterations or repair	Competent person, normally manufacturer	Form 97	At least every 6 months, except when used only occasionally
Wire rope	Before first use	Manufacturer	Form 87	At least every 6 months except when used only occasionally

Who carries out this work	Results to be recorded on Form No	Inspection to be carried out	Who carries out this work	Results to be recorded on Form No	Legal reference
examination		**C Inspection**			**D References**
		Weekly	Competent person, eg crane driver or fitter	Form 91 (pt I) E NOTE: this will be part of normaly weekly inspection	LO regn 30
		Weekly	Competent person, eg crane driver	Form 91 (pt I) E NOTE: this will be part of normal weekly inspection	LO regn 30
Competent person	Form 91 (pt II) G-K or on a special filing card containing the prescribed particulars	Weekly	Competent person, eg driver	Form 91 (pt I) C	LO regn 28 LO regn 10
Competent person, eg insurance company engineer	Form 91 (pt II) G-K or on special filing card containing the prescribed particulars	Weekly	Competent person, eg fitter	Form 91 (pt I) H	LO regn 46
Competent person eg insurance company engineer	Form 91 (pt II) G-K or on special filing card containing the prescribed particulars	Weekly	Competent person, eg fitter	Form 91 (pt I) F	LO regn 46
Competent person, eg insurance company engineer or at a testing house	Form 91 (pt II) J or on a special filing card containing the prescribed particulars	SPECIAL NOTE Chains or lifting gear which have to be annealed, see form 91 (pt I) for detail and LO 41		Form 91 (pt I) or form 1946 containing the prescribed particulars	LO regn 34 LO regn 40 LO regn 41
Competent person, eg insurance company engineer	Form 91 (pt II) J				LO regn 34

Continued. . .

Construction Operations *Continued. . .*

Type of plant equipment or job involved	A Testing and thorough examination			B Thorough
	Testing and thorough examination	*Who carries out this work*	*Results to be recorded on Form No*	*Thorough examination*
Steam boiler (new)	Before use	Manufacturer or boiler inspecting company	No special form	
Steam boiler (cold)				Every 14 months and after expensive repairs
Steam boiler under pressure				Every 14 months and after extensive repairs
Steam receivers and containers	Not required		A certificate as to the safe working pressure provided by maker	At least every 26 months
Air receivers	Before use	Manufacturer or insurance company engineer	A certificate as to the safe working pressure provided by maker	At least every 26 months (see special conditions)

NOTE
Abbreviations used
FA 1961   Factories Act 1961
WP regn   Construction (Working Places) Regulations 1966
GP regn   Construction (General Provisions) Regulations 1961
LO regn   Construction (Lifting Operations) Regulations 1961

Definition of lifting appliance
means a crab, winch, pulley-block or gin-wheel for raising or lowering and a hoist, crane, sheer-legs, excavator, dragline, piling-frame, aerial cableway, aerial ropeway or overhead runway.

Definition of lifting gear
means a chain, sling, rope-sling or similar gear and a ring, hook plate, clamp, shackle, swivel and eye bolt.

Competent person
There is no legal definition. The person who is selected or appointed to act as a competent person must have practical and theoretical knowledge together with actual experience on the type of plant, machinery, equipment or work which he is called upon to examine.
    Such knowledge and experience will enable him to detect faults, weakness, defects, etc, which it is the purpose of the examination to discover and assess.

NOTE
For other tests, examinations and inspections in connection with specialised operations, such as diving, work in compressed air, ionising radiations, etc, expert advice should be sought.

examination		C Inspection			D References
Who carries out this work	*Results to be recorded on Form No*	*Inspection to be carried out*	*Who carries out this work*	*Results to be recorded on Form No*	*Legal reference*
					FA 1961 s 33
Competent person, eg insurance company engineer	Form 55				FA 1961 s 33 (4)
Competent person, eg inusrance company engineer	Form 55A				FA 1961 s 33
Competent person, eg insurance company engineer	Form 58				FA 1961 s 35
Competent person, eg insurance company engineer	Form 59				FA 1961 s 36

EXEMPTIONS
Crawler-tracked shovel or dragline excavators
Such machines are occasionally used as cranes solely by the attachment of lifting gear to the shovel or bucket for work immediately connected with excavations the machine has been directly engaged on; this is only permissible provided a competent person specifies the maximum load or loads to be lifted. The maximum load or loads and the lengths of jib or boom to which they relate, together with a means of identification, must be plainly marked upon the excavator. The Certificate – Form 2209 – must be completed.

Legal reference:
FA 1961: The Construction (Lifting Operations) Regulations 1961 – Certificate of Exemption No. 2 (General).

The forms mentioned for result recording are those prescribed and are available from HMSO

The plant schedule is of obvious advantage to the site but for comparing management information systems will be necessary to assist in planning the whole plant function. Here senior management will require information such as:

- Plant asset registers which will provide information on the numbers, type, value and depreciation of existing plant stock.
- Plant utilisation reports. As has been mentioned the key factor in plant economics is the actual rate of utilisation. The greater the use the lower the unit costs of owning the plant. Consequently records which show the actual usage against the planned usage will be essential information when planning for a plant fleet. If utilisation in a particular type of plant (say tower cranes) is consistently low then this may direct the holding policy to hire in rather than hold tower cranes.
- Plant maintenance reports. Such information will again be vital to the plant department and each piece of plant or type of plant should have a maintenance record. This record could include the defects occurring and the number of hours down-time suffered. The records of plant performance in this area can help to shape the policy to maintenance. There will be several policy options available to manage the maintenance function and these will range from planned maintenance which may be preventative and corrective maintenance. Or plant maintenance may be unplanned and require attention or running repairs at the site. Clearly the planned maintenance option may be most desirable in that it minimises disruptive breakdowns but has the consequence of requiring extensive facilities which may prove expensive. Also the logistics of setting up networks of workshops to service geographically dispersed plant may be prohibitive. A more realistic policy may be to have local servicing arrangements with plant distributors.

Clearly these information requirements are best set up within the framework of a management information system which provides the feedback to determine the type and range of inputs being fed into the plant management sub-system.

To conclude the way in which the plant resource is managed will have a significant inpact upon the productivity achieved by the sites. Effective management of this resource is likely to be a key determinant of corporate success.

Questions

1 A building company has a plant department which provides the majority of mechanical plant and power tools for its sites.

   Consider the implications for the company of a proposal to re-form the department as a plant hire company.

   CIOB Part I *Building Management I* (resit) 1986

2 Many building organisations operate a flexible plant acquisition policy by owning some items of plant and hiring others.

   Discuss the implications of such a policy for plant management at site level.

   CIOB Part II *Building Management II* Paper 1 (resit) 1986

3 Evaluate the impact that mechanical handling has had upon the building process. What changes have been observed as a result of the greater use of mechanical plant?

4 A contractor has no plant department; each site manager is responsible for analysing plant needs and obtaining the necessary plant. Whilst this policy has worked well in the past there have been increasing difficulties with the provision of plant leading to delays and inefficient workings on some jobs. Write a report to the Managing Director of the company pointing out the drawbacks of the current system of obtaining plant for the site and advocate the introduction of a central plant department for the firm.

5 Managing the Inputs: Finance

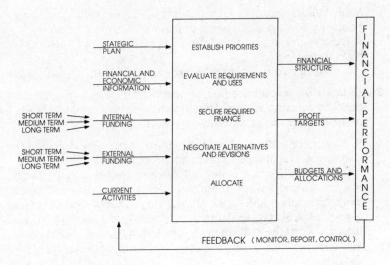

5.1 The financial system

5.1 Primary Task

The Primary Task is:

> To ensure that the necessary amounts of finance, of the appropriate types and mix, are available as and when required to permit the most efficient operation of the organisation and controlling the use of funds to ensure their effectiveness.

5.2 Introduction

Cash flow has been identified as the 'life-blood' of the construction industry. Although cash and its management are very important, other facets of financial management are vital to the success of any construction organisation.

Figure 5.1 depicts the financial sub-system of a construction organisation. Inputs to the system comprise the organisation's strategic plan, which provides overall guidance in terms of the organisation's objectives, etc, (see Volume 1 chapter 3); funding of short, medium and long term types obtained from sources both external and internal to the organisation; financial and economic information; current activities of the organisation. Together, the inputs provide demands for and provisions of finance in the contexts of the organisation's goals and the prevailing and anticipated economic and financial 'climates'.

The conversion processes are concerned with evaluating the demands for finance, matching those to the available funds and allocating the most suitable finances to the uses which will serve the organisation's objectives best.

The outputs from the sub-system are the financial structure of the organisation, which is a function of the organisation type, objectives, activities, available finances and costs thereof; profit targets for the organisation and its components (departments; projects, etc) and budgets and allocations of finance. The total outcome is financial performance which may be measured in various ways, eg profitability; size of asset base.

The feedback process contains some of the best known and widely practiced features of the system. Its purpose is to monitor and to provide data and information about the system's perfor- mance in order to facilitate control; in so doing it uses accountancy. Financial control is essential, especially to ensure that adequate cash is available. Lack of liquidity (cash and 'near cash') is the major cause of bankruptcies and liquidations in the construction industry.

5.3 Inputs

Strategic plan

The strategic plan of the organisation sets out the objectives which the organisation attempts to achieve through its activities. The financial sub-system can be regarded as one of the facilitating sub- systems in that it is not productive of itself but enables production to occur. Although the organisational form will have been determined when the organisation was set up, the strategic plan may contain proposals to alter the form and thereby affect the sources of finance available to the organisation. Also, the strategic plan may contain objectives concerning growth, profitability, asset structure and activities of the organisation; several of the objectives will have a direct bearing on the organisation's finances and should, where possible, be quantified in financial terms (amounts/and or ratios). Other objectives will have financial implications. Thus, whilst the nature of the organisation is an environmental (or contextual) factor, the contexts of the strategic plan set out directions and targets.

English law dictates that some forms of funding are unavailable to certain types of organisation. Neither sole traders nor partnerships can issue either shares or debentures. The number of and provisions for transfers of shares in private companies are rather restrictive. Larger public companies (PLCs) with full stock exchange quotations enjoy access to the widest spectrum of funds.

Although large, established companies enjoy widest access to funds and, due to their perceived greater security, may obtain funds relatively cheaply, there are certain special sources of finance which are devoted to small and/or new organisations. Many of the special sources of funds have been established recently following initiatives from Government. Several schemes focus on aspects of economic regeneration – to encourage organisations to locate in depressed inner urban areas; to foster new businesses, especially those started by unemployed people; to encourage people to invest in new/small businesses. Some schemes provide funds (often at the lower end of commercial rates of interest whilst) others encourage certain types of investments through tax incentives.

During the early-mid 1980s, the UK Government phased out allowances against Corporation Tax for companies' investments; in consequence, the rates of Corporation Tax were reduced. It was argued that such action forced companies to invest on the basis of 'real' costs rather than to gain tax advantages. The counter argument was that the policy discouraged investments by companies in new equipment and premises and so would hinder economic advancement. It is too early to determine which argument was correct.

Financial and economic information

Financial information is a sector of economic information which is concerned with availabilities, costs and uses of funds (money). Financial and economic information is generated by an enormous number of sources external to the organisation. Normally, organisations generate financial and economic information of their own – from their annual accounts to sophisticated and extensive research projects producing elaborate forecasts.

With the vast array of information available, a considerable amount of which is published daily, a major problem is the selection of the information which will be the most useful. Such information must be comprehensible, relevant and timely. Comprehensible by the decision takers in the organisation, relevant to the organisation's activities (present, future, and, sometimes, past – to provide explanations) and timely to facilitate action – forecasts or information used to produce forecasts.

The nature of available information varies from very general, eg Gross National Product, to very specific, eg cost of employing a labourer for a typical hour. Construction organisations use a broad spectrum of financial and economic information, the general pertaining to their environment, eg bank base rates; mortgage lending rate(s), industry level information, eg building cost indices; tender price indices; NEDO indices for the calculation of fluctuations, more specific being organisation level information, eg companies annual accounts, project level information, eg cost value reconciliations, and the most specialist being activity and operational level information, eg cost per m^2 of, specified, carlite plastering to a block wall on project 'X'.

The financial and economic information which constitutes an input to the financial sub-system will be an output of the organisation's information sub-system (see Volume 1 chapter 5).

Internal funding
Internal funding is finance provided by the operations of the organisation itself. In finance, periods are described based upon standard durations, short term – up to about three years, medium term – three years to twelve years, long term – over twelve years. Finance is generated internally by organisations relating to all three periods.

It is an all too common misconception that funding provided from internal sources is free, ie provided at zero cost; this is totally untrue. The cost of internal funding is its opportunity cost, the earnings which the funding would have generated in its next best use (assuming funds are directed to their best use – that which produces the highest return).

Short term internal funds are generated by mechanisms such as paying wages and salaries in arrears. The action generates credit for the organisation of (assuming linear value of production over time) the total of the arrears for half the arrears period (or half the arrears for the full period). A variety of internal charges which are settled periodically produce such funding, eg internal plant hire.

Internal, medium term funding is less common. A form used quite often is inter company loans within a group or loans to a sole trader's business by the individual (for a sole trader there is no legal differentiation between the business and the owner).

Long term, internal funds most often are provided by retained earnings. Retained earnings (or retained profits) are post-tax profits which are kept within the organisation (rather than being paid to the owners, such as by dividends to shareholders). Retained earnings form an important source of funds for expansion and for take-overs (it is common for a company to grow by taking over another company).

External funding

External funding is finance provided by sources outside the organisation, eg banks. The cost of the finance is visible immediately – it is the rates of interest charged.

There are many sources of external funding. Their availability to the organisation is determined by the primary factors of:

(a)   the organisation's form (sole trader, partnership, PLC, etc)
(b)   the purpose for which the funding is required
(c)   the period for which the funding is required
(d)   the level of risk associated with the funding, if provided.

Although funding bodies have been established with aims of providing finance to new/small organisations and/or to fund 'high risk' ventures, it is still the general case that large corporations and low risk activities enjoy greater access to funds. Co-incidentally, such organisations and activities obtain funds at relatively low cost.

Apart from the effects of supply and demand conditions which pervade the capital market in capitalist economies, the cost of finance capital (the rate of interest charged) is determined by:

(i)   the time period $\Big\}$ regarding the purpose for which the
(ii)   the risk   funding will be used
(iii)   inflation

Combination of the three factors (by addition or, preferably, by multiplication) yields the market or nominal rate of interest whilst the combination of factors (i) and (ii) yields the real rate of interest. The shorter the time period, the lower the (perceived) risk and the lower the rate of inflation, the lower the rate of interest.

Construction organisations undertake a variety of activities and types of projects. The activities generate differing requirements for funds, eg building contracting generates cash through the system of monthly (or, sometimes, more frequent) interim payments; property development requires considerable amounts of medium to long term funding to provide land banks plus short term funding to finance the development work.

Within the context of the financial structure necessary for the organisation to carry out its chosen activities, the main arbiter used to decide the sources of funding employed is cost; less expensive funding being preferred.

Where funding is obtained by offering capital accumulation such as by selling debentures at discount, ie at a price below their redemption sum, the cost of that funding must take such factors into account as well as the interest payable periodically.

Once the sources of external funding have been selected and the funding has been provided, there is likely to be a degree of inertia (to changes in the funding pattern). However, changes will occur to reflect alterations in the organisation's activities. For short term funding in particular, eg contractor's overdraft facilities, it is usual for the funding to be re-negotiated periodically to an extent that such financing is viewed as, effectively, a fairly permanent form.

External funding is obtained from the organisation's creditor's (as distinct from internal funding which is obtained from the organisation itself). Short term funding of construction contractors commonly is obtained from trade creditors (suppliers), Customs and Excise (VAT)[1], Inland Revenue (taxation)[1], banks (overdrafts and short term loans) and employees (wages, salaries and expenses). Medium term financing is obtained through medium term loans from banks and debenture holders (the latter are rather unusual). Long term financing is obtained through loans, often in the form of debentures. As the external suppliers of finance are creditors of the organisation:

(a) interest (and similar) payments to the creditors are business expenses and so are deductible against the organisation's taxation, thereby the cost of such finance is reduced, and

(b) if due payments are not made to the creditors, they have the power to seek liquidation of the organisation.

Uncertainty may be an important consideration in an organisation's seeking funding from external sources as such funds are obtained in the 'financial market place' and, therefore, are subject to the 'rigours' of market competition; the consideration is particularly pertinent to organisations which financiers perceive to be high risk, such as construction contractors.[2]

Gearing is the ratio of fixed interest finance to equity finance. As taxation renders a cost reduction on debt financing, a company will favour that cheaper source of funding. However, as gearing increases so do costs of the debt financing and the risks – the increased amount of debt funding produces a larger interest payment which, as an expense, must be met before any profits are available; the shareholders are at greater risk for the same reason.

---

[1] Taxation provides short term finance as tax settlements are made some time after the tax liability has been incurred (through earnings, etc.).

[2] *Note* Stock Market investments use the ß – ratio (the measure of an investment's sensitivity to market risk, it measures movements in the return on the particular investment relative to the return on a total market portfolio). $\beta > 1$ indicates sensitivity, the movement in the return on the particular share is more volatile than is the market generally, and vice-versa.

$r - rf = \beta\,(rm - rf)$

where: r = expected rate of return β = beta ratio
        rf = risk free rate of return rm = expected rate of
                                                 return on total
                                                 market portfolio.

Risky investments, such as construction, would be expected to have $\beta > 1$.

Further, if company income fluctuates the interest is a greater burden which may result in enforced liquidation if the charge cannot be met. Hence high gearing is not suited to construction organisations but is suited to organisations which operate in stable environments.

Current activities

An organisation's current activities are the main influence upon its financial system. They determine current and some future financial requirements in both quantity and mix. Construction contracts, via interim payments, are good generators of cash. Thus, in multi-activity organisations, contracting is used to provide liquid funding for other activities.

Current activities are the fruition of yesterday's plans (forecasts). In comparing plans and actual events it is important to note any differences and the reasons for such differences – particularly whether differences are within the plans margins of variability, are due to errors in the plans or are due to changed circumstances between the planning and execution stages. Allowance for a pre-determined degree of possible variability, eg ± 2 standard deviations, should be made in securing the funding necessary for the organisation's programmed activities to attempt avoidance of financial difficulties. The ways in which activities' financial requirements/performances inter-relate will be an important factor in calculating the 'safety net' allowance for variability. Such consideration is of particular importance to construction contractors in their negotiations of overdraft facilities.

The inputs concerning the organisation's current activities comprise:

(a)   plans of what is intended, and
(b)   feedback of what has occurred.

Both pieces of information are vital to the determination of the organisation's financial requirements and the allocation of available funds. Timeliness of the information is critical.

It is important that an organisation's financial system should be sufficiently flexible to cope with quite sudden and possibly large changes in actual performance from that which was predicted. Allowances for sources of variabilities (as noted above) should not be expected to be adequate for all eventualities, eg major industrial disputes; liquidations of important clients/suppliers/sub-contractiors, the variabilities for which provisions are made represent the organisation's balance between risk reduction and the cost of risk reduction (by marginal analysis, the benefit of a further increment of risk reduction is less than the cost incurred to achieve that increment – see figure 5.2). However, flexibility has a price if

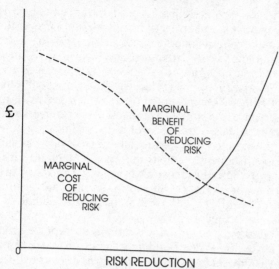

5.2 Effects of risk reduction. By marginal analysis, the optimal level of risk lies where the two curves equate

only in terms of opportunity costs so, despite the criticisms which may be levelled at it, a utility approach will allow the various requirements of the organisation to be taken into account to determine the appropriate level of risk and, hence, the form and flexibility of the financial system (see, for example, FELLOWS *et al.* 1983, pp 225–231).

Whilst construction contracts are generators of cash flow for contractors they also are consumers of finance. Cash flow analyses of construction projects (using 'typical' S-curve models) demonstrates that, upon translating the cash flow pattern into financial requirements (plots of gross and net cash flow curves, noting break even points), much short term and medium – long term finances are required as projects rarely break even until late in the contract period – see figures 5.3 and 5.4.

Certain techniques are employed to alter the cash flow patterns to achieve earlier break-even and to reduce the financial requirements of projects. Good credit control is the most effective technique (FELLOWS (1982)) followed by front end loading[1] item prices and securing as large cash inflows as possible via interim certificates (sometimes via dubious manipulations of valuations), especially early certificates.

---

[1] Front end loading involves pricing items of work which will be executed early in the contract period such that they include a disproportionately large amount for profit, prices of items executed later are reduced commensurately so as to maintain a constant contract sum.

Construction projects' prices must cover the direct costs of executing the work, the projects' overheads and a proportion of the organisation's general overheads, eg rent paid for head office; managing director's car. Direct costs are recovered via the prices of items of measured work (or similar). The project's overheads largely comprise items which are included in the Preliminaries section of Bills of Quantities, most of which are priced thereby providing recovery of those overheads. General overheads of the organisation usually are recovered by some pre-determined addition to estimated direct costs, labour costs or by an analogous mechanism – frequently employing a percentage upward adjustment to the predicted base cost. Overheads are allocated to projects and absorbed by them, therefore, in a somewhat arbitrary way which may not give a good reflection of the actual overheads devoted to the project.

However, the overhead allocation and absorption process is a practical necessity. When examining the financial performance of projects it is advisable to exclude the general overheads element and to consider that element separately in order that the actual financial performance of the projects are evaluated rather than, in part, the system of allocating overheads.

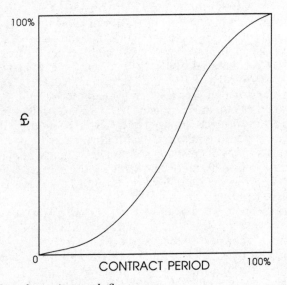

5.3   Simple project cash flow curve

Note   Alternative models produce curves of differing shapes (see, for example, HUDSON (1978)). The curve is a smoothed representation of the cash inflows to the contractor – the actual cash flow's being a stepped function. A similar analysis can be used for the contractor's cash outflows in which delays for making payments to suppliers, etc, can be incorporated easily.

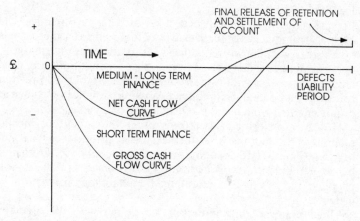

5.4   Typical project financial requirements
(ignores cash flows which occur prior to start on site)

5.4   Conversion process

The conversion process uses a variety of information and data inputs to produce the outputs. Success of the process is measured as financial performance via the feedback loop in the forms of absolute measures, eg amount of profit and comparative measures (against targets and/or other organisations' performances).

The organisation's environment plays a fundamental role in affecting the financial system through the availabilities and costs of the finances required by the organisation. The conversion process must be able to respond, often rapidly, to environmental changes – in extreme cases, failure to respond adequately will result in liquidation of the organisation. Thus, although the construction industry may enjoy some stability in that environmental influences are not of immediate effect due to the duration of construction contracts and leads through projects' design periods, the impact of the financial environment is likely to be rapid. To provide compensation, some standard contracts permit price fluctuations to be reimbursed but the impacts are not tackled in toto by such provisions.

The inputs which provide a long term view, notably the organisation's strategic plan, will be modified for expediency in the light of the inputs of shorter term natures. In that context, it is important to recall that decisions are forward-looking, the past comprises only 'sunk' events.

Establish priorities

For priorities to be established, a set of goals or objectives must exist. Normally, the objectives will be derived from the organisation's strategic plan with modifications to allow for alterations and prevailing circumstances – both of the organisation and of the environment. It is within the context of the established/prevailing priorities that demands for finance, possible supplies of finance and requirements for financial performance will be considered.

However, priorities take forms other than those of 'positive planning', the most obvious of these other priorities is what most organisations regard as being imperative – survival. During the buoyant periods of an organisation's existance, survival is not a problem and so other requirements dominate, eg profit; turnover; growth.

Thus, organisational imperatives together with the objectives contained in the strategic plan provide the basis on which tactics for development of the organisation, the pattern of activities which the organisation undertakes and how those activities are financed are founded. Given the objectives, the activities available to the organisation must be considered and projects and courses of action within those activity areas decided.

For most construction organisations, activities, projects, etc, which may be undertaken are constrained by the availabilities of financial and other resources. Therefore, it is important that the consequences of alternatives are evaluated and considered against the established priorities. As has been noted already, different construction activities have vastly different financial implications in terms of both financial input requirements and outputs.

An organisation's objectives may contain conflicts – for example, expansion of turnover may not be compatible with maximisation of profit in the short term. When establishing priorities and then placing them in a hierarchy it is helpful to note which are long term and which are short term; whilst the objectives themselves are likely to feature in both periods, their places in the hierarchies are likely to change as an organisation evolves.

Short term and, occasionally, longer term priorities/objectives of the organisation will alter over time. Normally the changes will be evolutionary as the organisation develops and adopts changes to its tactical and strategic plans; sometimes the changes must be revolutionary – rapid and sizable – caused by the necessity to respond to shocks in the environment (see also Volume 1 chapter 2).

The necessity to establish financial priorities is caused by two major factors:

(i)   financial performance often is used as the primary measure of an organisation's success, and

(ii)   availability of finance is restricted (this aspect is termed 'capital rationing').

The continuing existance of the organisation, especially in a highly capitalist environment, is dependent upon its achieving at least adequate financial performance (measured relatively – by comparisons with alternatives), which itself, in part, is determined by the success of the organisation's financial system in securing the required funds and doing so at minimum cost.

It is argued that modern financial markets, ie investors and their agents, eg fund managers, take an increasingly short term view; looking at returns on investments over months or a few years only to the exclusion of longer term effects. Such practice will bear upon construction organisations (perhaps especially upon developers and contractors) through requiring them to offer higher returns on the funds which they require.

The construction organisations, therefore, operate under considerable financial pressures (enhanced by the perceived riskiness of the industry); in such circumstances, the opportunities to subjugate the short term to longer term goals are constrained, eg the submission of a low bid to establish a relationship with a major, repeating client.

Thus the priorities must be kept under review to ensure that they accord with the organisation's objectives and the requirements of the environment.

Evaluate requirements and uses
Evaluation of the requirements for and uses of finance requires both measures and standards, eg the amount of profit and the level of normal profit. Due to capital rationing, inter alia, not all work opportunities will proceed – those which offer the highest returns will be selected first, those offering inadequate returns will be rejected, eg where the forecast return on investment for a project is less than the cost of financing that project. Some projects, which offer adequate but relatively low returns will be rejected also.

For construction organisations, the processes are complicated by the reliance which must be placed upon forecasts – notably of costs via the estimating and associated bidding procedures. No contractor can be certain of future workload (or its costs and profitability). Organisations have workload targets – usually expressed as turnover – and bid levels are adjusted in attempts to achieve those targets.

The intended uses of finance give rise to the requirements for finance. As figure 5.4 demonstrates, construction projects require finance over much of the construction period and become self financing and profitable only towards the end of construction. The mix of short term and long term finance which a project requires is determined by the nature of the work, how it is organised and the contractual provisions (particularly those relating to payments).

Almost invariably, projects may be constructed by several alternative methods, eg steel or rc frames; labour or capital intensive methods, be organised in different ways, eg design and construct or 'traditional'; use directly employed resources or sub-let most tasks, and be subject to various contractual terms, eg management contract; cost-plus contract of JCT 80; stage payments or monthly payments. The more frequent the payments to the contractor and the lower the contractor's investment (of various own resources) in the project, the lower the contractor's requirement for short term finance to execute the project will be. Use of 'up front' payments, such as the mobilisation fee which is common for international (FIDIC) contracts, are of great assistance in reducing the contractors' financial needs for the projects.

Uses of finance are considered in terms of what the investments are expected to generate. Requirements for finance are the financial needs (to facilitate the uses) and are regarded in terms of availabilities and costs. Thus uses should aim to generate inflows to the organisation in excess of the outflows (actual or/and opportunity) arising from the associated financial requirements.

There is considerable debate over what method should be employed to select projects for financing in a situation of capital rationing. The greater the duration of a project, the more important it is that a discounting method be employed. The method of calculating a project's payback period (a method used quite widely) is simple and may provide a helpful 'initial filter' but has many, well-known faults.

A project's payback period is the time over which the net cash flow of the project achieves break-even, ie initial investment minus subsequent net cash inflows generated by the project equals zero. The method is improved by applying discounting to the cash flows.

Other investment appraisal techniques in common usage are internal rate of return (IRR) and net present value (NPV); both have advantages and critics, the net present value approach usually being preferred. A project's IRR is that rate of interest which, when used as the cash flows' discounting factor, equates the cash outflows and inflows for the project over its entire life (including initial investment and scrap costs and values). A project's net present value is calculated by applying a pre-determined discount factor to future cash flows (sometimes different cash flow types for a project require different discount factors). IRR gives the project's average return, NPV is more flexible – it can incorporate several discounting rates and re-investments. Both techniques consider all cash flows for the project and, hence, it is important to use only relevant cash flows – those which relate to the project (rather than those which exist anyway) and those which occur from the decision to proceed with the project, ie 'sunk' cash flows, those which occurred prior to the decision, are not relevant, thus an incremental approach to evaluation of the cash flows is useful.

Often taxation is a significant complicating factor in investment appraisals. Taxation may be included in the evaluations either by adjusting the discount rate (for NPV) or, preferably, by including the taxation cash flows at the predicted times of their occurrences in the calculations (see, for example, MERRETT and SYKES (1973), FELLOWS *et al.* (1983)).

Thus, the evaluations of financial requirements and the uses from which they are derived should occur in two ways:

(a) investment appraisal techniques – to assist selection of the 'best' uses, and hence, the required finance, and

(b) determination of the amounts of actual ('cash-type') finances required and the timings of those requirements.

An important feature of the requirements/uses evaluations is control of the finances to ensure reasonable constancy. If financial requirements fluctuate wildly it will be extremely difficult and expensive to ensure adequate provisions. Thus, it is a common aim to achieve financial resource balancing (as for physical resources). The balancing requires careful analyses of project phasings between projects of differing sizes, types and durations – as the financial requirements of certain projects decline, so the requirements of others grow resulting in an overall (approximately) constant set of financial requirements for the organisation. Of course, it is necessary to give separate consideration to short term and long term finances as they are obtained from different sources.

As 'financial smoothing' may be a facet of the capital rationing to which an organisation is subject, it may be necessary to adjust the timings of projects, or component activities, to achieve the necessary smoothing (maintain the financial requirements with the limits prescribed). Naturally, a buoyant financial market in which finances are readily available, will provide relaxation to capital rationing and/or the financial smoothing but at a cost (higher interest rate for the additional finance). Also widely, randomly fluctuating financial requirements may be perceived to indicate an unstable organisation, lacking control of its finances, with obvious consequences.

Secure required finance

Once the financial requirements are known, the finances are secured from the selected sources by fairly standard methods. Generally, external short term finance is secured via personal contact whilst long term finance is secured more impersonally. Securing finance from internal sources occurs within the organisation's financial sub-system and so the techniques depend on how the sub-system operates, subject to owners' approval as at shareholders' meetings particularly a company's annual general meeting (AGM).

Personal contact methods of securing finance involve discussions and negotiations; therefore they tend to be quite flexible. The impersonal mechanisms for securing finance often involve financial intermediary organisations which specialise in the matters involved, eg an issuing house. Where the public are involved in the impersonal methods, they are invited to provide funding based upon a prospectus issued by the company or intermediary – the most common areas are new share issues and issues of debentures; rights issues are direct to existing shareholders in a company and scrip issues concern financial restructuring of a company and not raising new finance.

Some finance is secured through arrangements to operate the business – these concern finance through obtaining periods of credit (the period of delay between a cost's being incurred and settlement of that account). Thus employees via wages and salaries payment methods, suppliers and sub-contractors provide various periods of credit, and, therefore, short term finance, to construction organisations. Taxation provides finance in a similar manner as the tax accounts (VAT, Corporation Tax, etc) are settled periodically, usually several months after the liabilities have been incurred.

Clearly, by its nature, long term finance, including retained profits and similar 'reserves', provides the basic funding for the organisation; as such, changes in the long term financing are quite infrequent. The amount of short term finance required is related to the organisation's level of activity; as that may change rapidly so the financing arrangements should be flexible. Some are 'self-adjusting', particularly the credit provisions, whilst others require fresh arrangements for provision, eg bank loans and overdrafts; it is here that the negotiating skills and interpersonal qualities of the system's personnel in securing the required finance are crucial to the success of the organisation. Finance is required in the right *amounts*, at the lowest *price*, for the right *period* and at the right *time* (APPT).

Negotiate alternatives and revisions

The negotiations of alternatives and/or revisions occurs:

(i) as an internal mechanism (primarily) concerning revisions to the proposed methods, etc, of executing current and future (potential?) projects – thereby altering their cash flows and financial requirements, and

(ii) in relation to external and internal funding providers to secure the necessary finances when required – this may take the forms of options or of facilities, as with a bank overdraft.

The cost of the various forms of finance often acts as the arbiter for selecting the provider or whether a project can proceed.

As in most instances of negotiations, the relative (perceived) strengths of the parties plays an important role – in securing flexibility, the finances and the costs thereof. The stronger (larger?) the construction organisation is, the better will be the terms relating to the finances that organisation obtains and, due to the greater sources available, the more flexibility that organisation has in obtaining the finances.

Negotiating of alternatives/revisions does place the party seeking those changes in a somewhat weaker position, especially if the other party is aware of the former's need for the finances and the desired changes – this is especially significant if an organisation is in financial difficulties!

Both internal and external negotiations occur on personal, face-to-face bases; this is in contrast with much securing of finance, especially long term, which occurs via impersonal prospectuses and via intermediaries. The negotiations concern the securing of short (to medium) term finance to meet some requirements at variance with those planned, eg a major contract is altered and delayed severely.

Naturally, it is wise for an organisation to keep alternative forms and sources of financing its activities under constant review in order to ensure that the required funding is obtained as effectively (especially as cheaply) as possible.

Allocate

Whilst much of the finance is secured on the basis of workload targets and so funding must be allocated to projects as the latter are obtained, some exceptional projects may arise from time to time which are of sufficient attraction to induce the organisation to seek that work in addition to the targeted workload. Such exceptional projects will require individual (incremental) financing and so finance is sought for that particular project alone rather than for general expected workload. The projects may become part of the organisation's general activities if, subsequently, they are obtained quite regularly (such as occurs when an organisation successfully expands its activities into a new sub-market).

Once finance has been secured, the sub-system must allocate the funds to the most appropriate uses. Whilst it is convenient to consider funds from long term sources financing fixed assets, one pound is identical to any other, and so, whilst the amounts involved will relate, the use of each unit of finance (pound, etc) is independent of its source.

Superficially, it might appear that allocation of finance is a formality – intended target uses have led to procurement of funds which should then be directed to the secured activities/projects denoting those uses. However, the sub-system is subject to various dynamics in that financial requirements and availabilities may change rapidly and in large measure – hence the need for a sensible size of 'reserves'[1] or 'safety net'. The size and composition of the 'safety net' should be determined by statistical methods as holding funds available for use has a cost and so the size of the safety net should be as small as possible commensurate with its objective.

Considerations for allocations of finance between uses in situations of capital rationing (limited supplies of finances) have been noted above. It is important that such objective techniques are used for allocations, rather than to allocate on the basis of subjective guesses, to ensure best allocations (best in the sense of most likely to contribute most towards the achievement of the organisation's objectives). It is vital that allocations be based on evaluations; even in instances where funds are limited and, consequently, cost appears to be the dominant factor, it is still the relation (surplus) between revenue and cost which should determine the uses of the available funds.

5.5 Outputs

The purpose of the financial sub-system is to produce the outputs which maximise the organisation's financial performance. Whilst the accounting view tends to be short term, the economist's view places considerable importance on longer terms due to their portrayal of underlying factors (economic, demographic trends, etc). Normally, financial performance is measured via accountancy and so considers the accounting period (usually a year). However, by reviewing several years' accounts a longer term picture, revealing trends, can be established.

Financial structure
An organisation's financial structure is the framework within its financial activities occur. The structure is rather fixed in the short term but should be one which evolves to suit the organisation's changes in objectives, activities and environment.

It is useful to regard an organisation's financial structure as an

---

[1] Reserves in this sense, to attempt to obviate financial problems, must not be confused with the reserves which are noted on balance sheets; the latter are funds retained within the organisation instead of being distributed to owners (or other claimants).

element of facilitating mechanism rather than as an independent 'end in itself'. The structure must be appropriate to the organisation's activities; the activities, current and future, determine the finances required. In essence the structure is the best mix of short, medium and long term funding for the organisation but, within that outline matrix, the primary determinants of the sources from which the funds are obtained are the availabilities and costs of those funds.

Property companies, component manufacturers and similar operations, which require large amounts of fixed capital, need a financial structure which contains a large proportion of long term financing. Contractors usually do not have a vast array of fixed assets (as a proportion of total assets), their current assets form a considerable part of their total assets, and, therefore, these organisations require a financial structure which places emphasis on short and medium term finances.

An organisation's working capital is a vital component. Working capital is current assets minus current liabilities and, as such, is current assets financed from long term liabilities (funding).

As it is common to evaluate financial performance through accounting ratios, so such ratios are of value also in examining an organisation's financial structure. Several ratios have 'universal' norms which indicate adequacy of performance, eg Current Ratio 1.5:1 to 2:1; Quick Ratio 1:1, whilst others have norms for an industry at a given time, eg P/E Ratios for ordinary shares, and others are particular to an organisation at a time, eg Working Capital Ratio. As such ratios are measures of financial performance when viewed against the organisation's financial structure, eg ratio of long term finances to total finances, they can be used to detect any weaknesses and advisable areas for restructuring.

Profit targets
Most organisations are strongly profit motivated; profit maximisation is an assumption about organisation objectives which, although somewhat crude, is applied widely. There may, of course, be some foregoing of short term profits to enhance longer term gains. Profit is a surplus, the surplus of total revenue over total costs (for the period). Naturally, it is helpful to an organisation for it to carry out more detailed analyses so that the sources of profits may be evaluated individually, eg property investments; plant hire, general contracting; management contracting, design services.

In the long term, an organisation must produce at least normal profit[1]. The level of normal profit depends upon risk levels, alternative investments, etc, and so may alter over time. Usually, organisations' profit targets will exceed the level of normal profit

[1] Normal profit is that level of profit which is required over the long term to retain the owners' investments in the business.

but in the short period, organisations also have the flexibility to earn less than normal profit provided that over the long period, sufficient compensation of additional profit is earned.

However, whilst at the strategic level normal profit is an important consideration, at the tactical or operational level different approaches to profit targets apply. Such approaches for the organisation as an entity concern measures such as total profits before interest payments and taxation; total pre-tax profits; trading profit and the profits earned by individual divisions, activities etc of the organisation. For contractors, individual projects will have cost, revenue and, hence, profit targets.

The time dimension of profit is important, so it is usual for targets to be produced for a specified period. If an organisation undertakes many projects and, perhaps, carries out a variety of activities – plant hire, materials/component production, etc – subject to variations such as occur through the seasonal pattern of workload, profits will be obtained in a fairly linear pattern. The same cannot be said for individual projects, each will have its own pattern of profit accrual depending upon the pricing pattern adopted and the circumstances of the project. Even though each item on a project may be priced to contain the same (anticipated) percentage on cost for profit, and so profits should accrue (on paper) in accordance with the progress of the work, payments circumstances as per cash inflows and outflows (periodic payments, credit periods, retentions, etc) modify the pattern in which the actual profit is obtained. Patterns of accrual and realisation of expected profits and cash flows are important in monitoring projects' financial performance via mechanisms such as monthly cost-value reconciliations.

Budgets and allocations

Budgets are statements of what is required of projects, activities or organisations in financial terms. As such they demonstrate both expectations and limitations. Therefore, budget statements are important documents in the processes of financial control.

Allocations are the actual provisions of finances. The allocations must be controlled so that the flow of funds accord with the requirements of the projects, etc, and should also align with the budgets. Thus the allocations of finances are the organisations' internal processes for channelling funds to their pre-decided uses.

Budgets are complementary to the profit targets in that they denote the envisaged patterns of expenditure and incomes. The budgets may concern costs, revenues or investments and may consider those aspects either separately or in combination, eg combination of costs and revenues expected on a project to yield a cash flow budget.

5.6 Feedback

Parts of the feedback portion of an organisation's financial sub-system must be published if the organisation is of certain form, eg a public company. The publication is in the form of the organisation's annual accounts and reports annexed thereto. However, the majority of the feedback is internal to an organisation, including much of the work necessary to produce information for external use.

An organisation's accounts often form the basis for analyses of that organisation's financial performance, relative, absolute and over time. Trends form a mainstay of such analyses. However, several important factors pertaining to the use of such accounts should be noted:

1 A profit and loss account is a record of the organisation's financial activities for the period but the balance sheet is an *instantaneous* financial picture of the organisation.
2 To produce trends, it is advisable to use at least five years' accounts. The trends are likely to be valid for quite short periods only as they are accounting trends; economic, social, demographic, political, etc., forces are the real underlying variables of longer term influences.
3 Accounts are records, produced in accordance with legislation; although they provide information for predictions (trends, ratios) that is not their purpose.
4 Accounts are not 100% accurate, there is some flexibility in their production and contents as there is with director's reports.

Essentially the monitoring and reporting components of the feedback loop are the province of accountancy whilst the control element is managerial, based upon what the accounting has produced. Accounting is passive in that it depicts what has occurred but the notion of 'creative accounting' recognises that accountancy can depict the same situation differently, and thereby prompt different actions, whilst remaining within the discipline's rules and conventions. To be 'creative', the accountant must anticipate what actions would be likely to follow from the information provided and how the actions would differ depending upon permissible variations in that information; the final facet is appreciation of accounting to yield apparently different results from the same data. Thus the creative element is providing the information in a way which leads to the desired action's being taken.

Even within the context of creativity, accounting follows a variety of principles and conventions as well as essential techniques.[1] Transactions are recorded and reports are prepared using money as the unit(s) of measurement – usually ignoring any changes in the value of money over time. Historic cost accounting is used widely (items are recorded at their cost when purchased and subsequent adjustments are based upon that sum) but current cost (or inflation) accounting is gaining quite extensive use. Accounting must be consistent in order that comparisons over time and between organisations may be carried out; if a method is changed, results of the old and the new should appear together to maintain comparability. Accounting is conservative/prudent; within the accruals approach, liabilities are accrued as they appear but profits may not be incorporated until realised. Each business is treated as an entity and is regarded as a going concern (except in special cases such as liquidation accounting).

Monitor

The initial step in monitoring is to record. Within the financial subsystem recording is also the first element of the accounting process – all events which have a financial aspect are recorded in the organisation's books of accounts, eg day book; cash book; ledgers. Each transaction is recorded as it occurs; further aspects of the transactions may follow in stages, (eg a sale is made on credit; payment is received later). Every transaction has two, balancing aspects which are recorded as a debit entry and a credit entry in the organisation's accounts. A debit entry records the increase of an asset account or the reduction of a liability account whilst a credit decreases an asset account or increases a liability account. The process is double entry bookkeeping and is the origin of the balance sheet (for the sale which initially is on credit with the payment following:

1 debit debtors, credit sales
2 debit cash and credit debtors).

Production of accounts occurs in a hierarchical manner. Books of original entry (initial recording of transactions) are proved (checked for arithmetic accuracy) at frequent intervals (daily/weekly) before the process of posting – transferring the account entries to higher level accounts. Ultimately the accounts are summarised in the forms of profit and loss accounts and balance sheets, etc.

Normally, the process of monitoring focusses on a small number of key issues and measurements and will involve comparing performance with targets. The aim of monitoring is to detect any

---

[1] Details of accounting terms, principles, conventions and techniques are to be found in most accountancy textbooks. See also: FELLOWS *et al.* (1983).

variances and to do so as early as possible so that control action may be instigated effectively (see also Volume 1 chapter 5). It is helpful if the monitoring can determine/suggest the causes of the variances also.

Although certain key variables will apply to almost all organisations, eg profit, others will vary in importance depending on the types and activities of the particular organisation. For construction contractors, the cash cycle and control of cash, both amounts and flows, is of great importance. Shortages of cash (and 'near-cash') create major problems – inability to pay wages, creditors and so on; indeed lack of liquidity is the most common cause of liquidations, a factor of particular poignancy to construction – the industry which suffers the highest rate of bankruptcies.

A surplus of cash is rather undesirable also. Assets in the form of cash are not earning a return and so may have a high opportunity cost. Thus, any surplus cash should be invested, even if on very short term, eg overnight, at the extreme; in practice the organisation's bank may agree that current account balances above a predetermined figure will be transferred into a deposit account and sums may be transferred into the current account from deposit to maintain a certain balance. The objective is cash adequacy – always enough cash (liquidity), plus a small reserve, to operate the business smoothly.

Plans and records are important yardsticks against which current performance may be monitored. It is vital to recall that circumstances may alter and thereby detract from the validity of the plan; also plans themselves have inherent variabilities and/or just may be wrong.

Report (see also Volume 1 chapter 5)
Financial reports are part of the organisation's information subsystem as well as part of the financial system; they are prerequisites for control. Reporting communicates information, often upwards through the managerial hierarchy. It is a means by which a bulk of data/information is distilled to yield the essentials for decision taking.

Reports are best in standard formats for ease of understanding, use and comparisons. They may be provided at regular intervals, eg monthly cost-value reconciliations or occasional, they may inform of events and situations, eg profit and loss account; balance sheet, or inform of exceptions, eg variance reports. Several types of report may be used together to elicit further information but it is helpful if the reports themselves are identifiably individual/specific (use different headings, formats, colours of paper).

Control

Ineffective control is waste. For control to be effective, the decision takers must receive the necessary information at an appropriate time, understand the information and possibilities, possess the authority and have access to resources to take any action decided. Many of the requirements for effective financial control are facets of other sub-systems of the organisation and their impacts upon the financial sub-system, eg information; management. Understanding the information and possibilities requires knowledge of and expertise in accountancy and finance.

Control is action to modify performance to improve results. Thus, it is more than achieving targets. Variances may be positive as well as negative, although attention usually is focussed on negative variances with any positive ones accepted as good fortune. Often control sets out to achieve reductions in costs with targets being regarded as permitted maxima; here a feature of control may be that only minimal (if any) use is made of the available overdraft facility (provided that is the least cost policy).

In construction organisations, particular features of financial control are cash, credit and costs.

Tradition, and theoretical practice, suggest that construction project prices are cost-based with adjustments for profits in the context of the perceived market environment, other views assert that market forces dominate (see FELLOWS 1986). (*Note*: costs must be covered and normal profits earned, as a minimum, for an organisation to remain in business in the long term.) As the contract sum, initial price, is established at the outset of construction, contractors' control focusses on costs. The more work which is sub-let, the greater tends to be certainty of costs as the contractor can pass on many cost increases to obtain price increases, eg variations. Other cost increases are the sub-contractors risks. Some cost increases must be absorbed by the contractor, eg those caused by: inefficient work execution by directly employed operations; managerial inefficiencies causing poor organisation at the work-place, and it is those areas upon which most cost control naturally focusses. Clearly, control of costs to achieve reduction when the price is 'fixed' yields additional profit.

Most contracting organisations review costs on site at weekly intervals with reports to higher management less frequent. Such a procedure facilitates site cost control of activities (actions can be rapid).

Credit control has been demonstrated to be a principal factor affecting profitability of construction organisations, eg FELLOWS (1982). An organisation should not offer its customers better credit arrangements than it enjoys. Analyses of credit obtained and provided uses the ratios:

$$\frac{\text{Creditors} \times 12}{\text{Purchases}} \rightarrow \text{months credit enjoyed}$$

$$\frac{\text{Debtors} \times 12}{\text{Turnover}} \rightarrow \text{months credit offered}$$

Both figures are averages and usually employ data from the organisation's balance sheet. Wherever possible, an organisation should minimise the credit it offers whilst maximising the credit it obtains.

Two problems which arise with credit are that discount is limited directly to the credit period – if payment is not made within the prescribed period the discount is lost; 'inflation' may dominate any discount offered such that, due to costs of finance, it is cheaper to lose the discount to obtain a greater period of credit (which, in such situations, is cheap finance).

In construction, credit periods are widespread and of prescribed standards, often with associated discount arrangements. Credit control, whilst following the principles outlined above, must also ensure that through 'over-manipulations' the reputation/operations of the organisation are not damaged (as could occur through making very late payments to suppliers, etc, and so possibly suggesting that the organisation is in financial difficulties, even on the verge of liquidation).

Despite the industry's paying much attention to control of costs, credit and cash flows, settlement of final accounts is a notoriously lengthy process in which delays will, at least in part, offset the gains effected through good controls during the construction phase.

Therefore, it is advisable for organisations to pursue the settling of final accounts with vigour – it may be far more economic to settle a claim at a lower level to secure early payment than to establish entrenched stances resulting in 'bad feelings', delays in settlement and, utlimately, expenditure on arbitration or litigation (to the delight of lawyers).

Questions

1 (a) Examine the differences between Net Present Value (NPV) and Internal Rate of Return (IRR) methods of investment appraisal.

   (b) A building developer is considering an office development at a cost of £8 million. The predicted annual rental is £900,000 for the first 20 years, and £700,000 for the next 20 years. Rent will be paid one year in advance. The life of the building will be 40 years, with a residual value (after demolition costs have been taken into account) of £2 million. All the values assume constant prices. Finance is available at 11%.

Calculate the NPV and IRR for this development. Make recommendations on the basis of the calculations including any necessary reservations.

CIOB *Building Economics and Finance* 1988

2 Explain why building companies require short term finance and examine its types and sources.

CIOB *Building Economics and Finance* 1988

3 Examine the role of budgets in the management and control of building activities.

CIOB *Building Economics and Finance* 1987

4 Explain how cash flow for a contractor differs from that of a developer and relate this to the need to raise finance. Discuss the sources from which such funds may be obtained.

CIOB *Building Management I,* 1986

6 The Production Sub-system

6.1 Introduction

The focus of this chapter is the aspect of construction which is given considerable attention – production. This is the task of most construction companies and in managing such organisations the need to maintain and improve production is frequently emphasised. The task of 'constructing' may be seen as the primary purpose of construction firms and to obtain production some resources have to be inputted to a system and converted by managerial action into the physical product. This system approach is again used to analyse the production sub-system but in this case the outputs of other sub-systems become the inputs to this sub-system. Figure 6.1 gives an overview of the system to be used in this chapter.

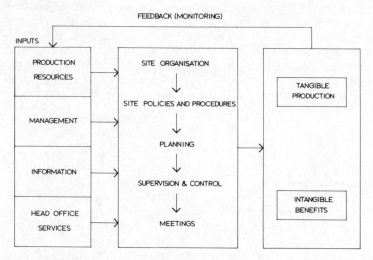

6.1   A systems model for the production sub-system

As can be seen the inputs to the system can be physical resources such as plant, materials, labour and finance and these will be drawn into the sub-system from their own sub-systems. Chapters 2, 3 and 4 discuss these resources. Not only will the quantity of these resources be important but the quality and timing of their intervention be crucial to the satisfactory performance of the primary task of the sub-system. Other resources will also have to flow into the system; Management will have to be provided with the appropriate amount of information and head office services may be required to sustain the management processes carried out on site. These resources will flow through a process operated by site management. The site organisation set up will reflect the nature of the site, its size, its location, the type of project etc and this will shape the division of work between site and head office. This organisation structure will inform the policies and procedures which in turn will shape the type, style and amount of supervision and control exercised on site. Meetings will be used to monitor the fluency of the flow of these resources through the site. Finally the outputs will be physical production which will be tangible and such intangible outputs such as client and user satisfaction for the building, the experience gained by the contractor and enhanced reputation and capacity for the builder and the sub-contractors.

For purposes of this chapter the boundary to the system is defined by spacial aspects – where the resources are used. In construction the production process takes place largely on sites and the system boundary is set by the site activity. The activities carried out at head office, suppliers, manufacturers plants, etc, are said to be outside the system although the actions of others will have a profound effect upon the inputs to the sub-system. In particular the physical resources which provide much of the inputs are supplied from outside the system but failure to supply in time has a profound effect upon the tasks undertaken in the conversion process stage and the final output of the system. The feed-back loop from the output to the inputs attempts to monitor and rectify if necessary any shortcomings in the input phase of the system.

6.2 Inputs

Production resources
Here physical resources such as labour, plant, materials and finance are brought into the system. Each resource will have its own sub-system and in line with classical systems theory the outputs of the manpower sub-system (chapter 2), the plant sub-system (chapter 4), the materials sub-system (chapter 3) and the financial sub-system (chapter 5) will become the inputs to the production sub-system. These chapters should be read for a fuller coverage of this input.

Information
Here the inputs can be broken into two parts – that provided as part

of the design information and that which is part of the contractors own data. The former will include formal contract documents such as the drawings, the specification and the Bill of Quantities. The latter will include data used for the contractor's own purposes. The method statement, the programme, the tender analysis, experience of local conditions and simple know how etc will be examples of the latter.

Such information is again part of the information/communications sub-system and this is covered in Volume 1 chapter 5. However, it would be useful to point out that the information input is the resource which is frequently cited as the most problematic for site management to handle. Poorly co-ordinated information has led to a major research theme of co-ordinated project information with initiative being taken by the Department of the Environment (1971) and the Co-ordinating Committee for Project Information (1987). This research effort was stimulated by a recognition that information black-outs often occur because of the complex arrangements of organisations which contribute to the building process. Thus, formal information is frequently supplemented by informal communication networks such as 'phone calls, impromptu meetings, chance encounters, etc, evinced by the Tavistock (1966) report.

In practice this combination of formal and informal information provides the material with which site management can develop the product of the production sub-system.

Head office services
The work of the production sub-system has to be enhanced by the inputs from the head office of the inputs to the sub-system and the strength and impact of this input will vary with the organisation and structure of the company and the strategy which it is pursuing. Crudely put the greater the sense of decentralisation, the greater will be the autonomy of the sites to manage the production sub-system. However, in any arrangement it will be likely that some of the following services will be provided by head office:

- Safety management
- Planning
- Buying/Estimating
- Land surveying
- Work study
- Wages administration
- Training, Personnel and Industrial relations
- Quantity surveying.

The personnel who provide such services to the site may be defined as undertaking *staff* activity – they exist to make the work of the production sub-system more effective. The work at the site level is that which is directly related to the objective of making a building grow – this is called a *line* activity. The work of the site in the production sub-system is easily recognisable but the work of *staff* services is less direct but equally important. Such staff activities reflect the 'line and staff' approach to structuring organisations. In its basic form the firm is divided into functions such as administration, estimating, contract management (although product or geographical divisions are also possible). An example of line and staff organisation is shown in figure 6.2.

The staff activities may be divided into two groups:

(a)   specialist staff
(b)   personal staff.

The specialist staff work with site managers to provide expert advice. Personal staff are attached to particular managers to carry out routine tasks or undertake task-force type work on behalf of the manager.

Within construction organisations the incidence of personal staff may be small and this discussion focuses upon the specialist staff. The specialist staff at head office may be sub-divided into four types. They are:

– advisory staff
– service staff
– control staff.

Advisory staff
This group of staff prepares plans for the site manager in his/her area of specialism but the site manager has no obligation to follow the recommendations. An example in a building organisation would be a training manager advising the site manager to run in-house seminars for junior staff in contractual matters. It is up to the site manager to accept or reject the advice. Put short it is up to the advisory staff to 'sell' not 'tell' their services to the site managers.

Service staff
As its name implies this is a staff group which services the production sub-system but is distant from the site management. An example in a building organisation would be the buying function. The site manager knows what is required but he/she has to go through the 'buying' department in order to place the order. Inevitably this process restricts the autonomy of the site but the specialist skills of say, the buying department are obtained.

Control staff
Here the term refers to a staff group which have responsibility for controlling certain aspects of the performance of the production

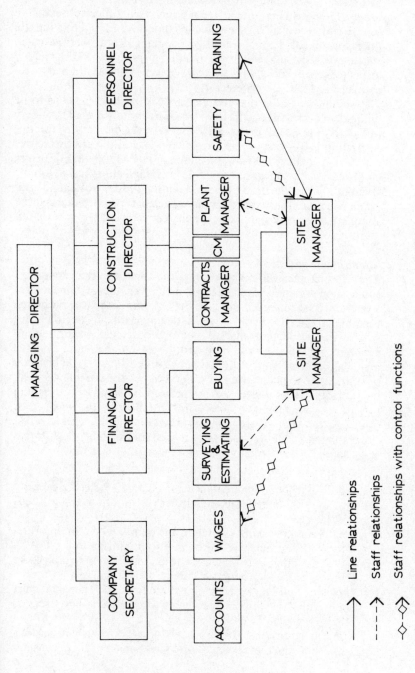

6.2 *Line and staff organisation chart*

sub-system. An example from a building organisation would be the input from the safety officer. Here if the safety officer observed an unsafe situation then he/she would be empowered to direct the site manager to correct it. A further example from contractors in speculative housing would be quality inspectors. If the quality inspector spots something which is not acceptable then the site manager is deemed to correct it.

It should be noted that the authority of such staff needs to be limited to control of specific functions. So the authority of the safety officer is limited to issues affecting safety. The reason for this restriction is obvious in that excessive power exercised by control staff can cut across chains of command. Despite this difficulty control staff have a useful function in establishing and enforcing standards across the organisation. Additionally control staff play an important part in co-ordinating specialist activity across the company, eg safety standards, quality control, etc.

Management input

The site manager will make an important input to the production sub-system for the site manager is a top manager within the site 'system'. He/she has, according to FRYER (1985), 'the job of welding together an effective team, as well as dealing with outside influences such as the local labour market, competitors, local authorities and suppliers. The manager may regard the design team and even his own head office as outside forces which make demands on him that are difficult to meet'. The tasks undertaken by the site manager will be discussed under the section on the conversion processes but the *role* of the site manager will be influential upon the success, or otherwise of the production system. HATCHETT (1971) sees effective site management being based upon a need for flexibility, he lists five skills as essential ingredients for site managers. They are:

(a) negotiation skills
(b) skills associated with engineering change – here the capacity for the site manager to align other organisations to the needs of the site
(c) match-making skills – matching the people who want information with those who have the required information.
(d) team building skills – to build the necessary team to undertake the work of the production sub-system
(e) skills of bending rules – on occasion the site manager must bend rules to overcome problems which no one party sees as their responsibility.

HATCHETT agrees that exercising this skill is obviously hazardous but it is a skill which many successful site managers have learned.

6.3 The conversion process

The site organisation
The resources identified will flow through the conversion processes of the site management system. The key to the conversion process is the organisation structure of the site. Earlier the traditional 'line and staff' organisation structure was briefly discussed. Other organisational structures are of course available and in many building projects mature organisation structures are desirable given the large number of different participating organisations. This point is made more fully in chapter 4 – the structural sub-system.

The structure of the site organisation will reflect the characteristics of the building project – its size, the type of projects in terms of technical complexity, the form of contract being used and the type of staff available to service the project. Finally the services from the Head Office will need to be reflected in the site organisation. Frequently the site organisation is expressed as a chart and such instruments can do much to identify 'who does what'. However useful organisation charts are, they have limitations in that they emphasise hierarchy and do not reflect the subtleties of informal relationships essential to the work of the production sub-system. Figure 6.3 illustrates a typical organisation chart for a medium sized site using a traditional form of contract.

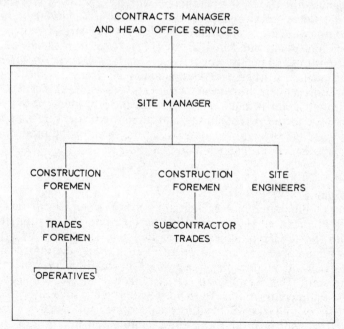

6.3   Typical organisation chart

Site policies and procedures

Supporting the formal organisation of the production system are the policies and procedures used on the site. In many ways the work of the site will be less governed by rules and procedures than larger, more bureaucratic organisations. However, questions such as:

- Who can authorise overtime working?
- What is the declared hard-hat area?
- How are consumables issued?
- What are the procedures in the event of an accident on site?
- What is done on receipt of drawing revisions?
- What is done upon receipt of architects instructions?
- What is to be done when insufficient, unclear or contradictory contract information is noted?
- What is to be done to receive materials on site?

Such issues can be documented and by doing so the site organisation goes some way to ensuring that tasks are allocated and performed in a routine way. They can make routine decisions automatically and thus protect the site manager from making decisions on many minor matters.

The most prominent form of rules and procedures used on site is in the area of industrial relations. In some senses this is regulated by the legal environment with its precedents and codes of practices but some firms have chosen to codify their own industrial relations procedures by using 'Procedure Agreements' to supplement the National Working Rule Agreement. Such procedure arguments would cover matters such as discipline, redundancy, working practices, manning levels, etc.

Before leaving the section on rules and procedures it is advisable to sound a note of caution. Site policies and procedures need to be relevant to the particular site and monitored to ensure that the policies and procedures are assisting the work of the production sub-system rather than hampering it.

Planning

During the preparation of the tender the pre-contract programme will be prepared and in most contracts the programme submitted with the tender becomes part of the contract documents. This programme will be developed further following the award of a contract and this document is a primary source of information to the site staff. The overall plan sets the standard of performance in respect of contract time for the production sub-system.

This overall plan will obviously need refinement so that it may be used to control production work. Unforeseen occurrences may distort the programme and particular work sections may necessitate reprogramming during the life of the contract. Moreover the overall plan is broadly based and this will need to be broken down into greater detail to effectively plan ahead. Here breaking down the overall plan with programmers with limited time horizons. Typical plans may be formed for:

- stage planning
- weekly planning
- daily planning.

Stage or short term planning
This is usually a plan for a few weeks' work or may be a detailed plan for a work section, eg foundations. This will break down the macro items listed on the overall plan and identify the specific resources required to undertake the work.

Weekly planning
This plan is directed to assist the trades to plan their work for the week. By planning for the week the trades foremen can be what is required of their group and establish a 'visible' target for the ganger or chargehand.

Daily planning
This is a breakdown of the weekly plan and will seldom be written down. More likely it is oral communication between the trades foreman and the chargehand. Obviously the daily activity will need to be related to daily allocation sheets which record the work done by particular gangs.

These plans establish the standards of time performance on the production sub-system. Other standards will also be set – budgets are obviously one key standard for the control of costs. This will link with the financial sub-system explained in chapter 5.

Supervision
Supervision is a part of the management of the production sub-system. Management effort is frequently defined as controlling operations and operatives who perform the work. This control may be undertaken in two ways by administration, eg setting plans, etc, and by direct overseeing of the work. The supervisors effort lies in the arena of direction and overseeing the work as done on site. It is an essential process if the inputs to the sub-system are to be effectively converted to outputs. TEMPORAL (1976) sees construction supervisors as having a four-way responsibility to operatives, to managers, to specialist departments and to other supervisors. He presents the relationship of the supervisor to others as shown in figure 6.4.

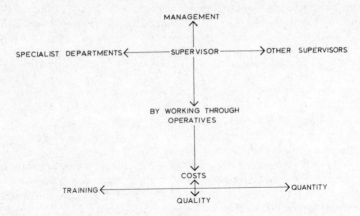

6.4   *Responsibilities of supervisors*

The supervisor is responsible for the processes which make the building grow on site. This model may be atomised to assist in the understanding of the supervisors role. HATCHETT (1976) identifies three factors associated with effective supervision, viz:

(a)   Concern for the task
(b)   Concern for the people doing the task
(c)   Concern for the co-ordination and control of the tasks and people.

The supervisors control the production sub-system and this imposes heavy responsibilities upon the supervisor. It is easy to advocate paragons for this job but the following itemises some good practice for supervision but recognises that these are subject to the human frailties which beset us all. In short the supervisor is responsible for getting work done and completing the job on time with the correct use of labour, materials and machines. So the manpower, materials and plant sub-systems relate strongly to the production sub-system through the supervisory function. In order to get the work done the supervisor will need to demonstrate three distinct abilities:

−   technical abilities
−   administrative abilities
−   human relations abilities.

The technical abilities covers the skills and knowledge which the supervisor needs to have in connection with the output for which he/she is responsible. For example, knowledge of the capabilities of various pieces of plant on the site and the knowledge of the skills required to operate these machines and tools.

The administrative abilities covers the clerical work involved on the project. For example, knowledge of the controlling and documentation procedures in the organisation. This will often involve documenting materials received, materials reconciliations, labour output and hours records, data for sub-contractor payment or incentives, etc.

The human relations abilities of a supervisor covers all the human aspects involved. This may be relationships with superiors, sub-ordinates and often colleagues. The quality of the human relations skill will be a key factor in handling the site, it will encompass communication skills in giving orders and instructions, talking to operatives, designers and clients – each requiring a different style and frequently a different vocabulary. Finally negotiation skills will be part of the battery of human relations ability.

The responsibilities of a supervisor on site may be expressed as a checklist. The supervisors responsibilities to the building organisation will include to:

- carry out the set policies
- ensure that set objectives are achieved, or, that information is passed on quickly, showing deviations or possible deviations to the plan
- ensure that materials arrive at the right time
- ensure that equipment and plant is available at the right time
- ensure the right man/machine balance
- ensure that the work is done in the objective time
- ensure that work done is to the right quality standard
- ensure that good relationships exist
- ensure effective communications exist, forward, backward and sideways
- ensure that the right men are put to the right jobs
- ensure that his men possess the right skills for the job they are doing . . . or . . .
- ensure that training programmes are designed to meet the need.

To the operatives that:

- some responsibility is delegated to them
- they know and understand what is expected of them in terms of quantity, quality and time
- the requirements of the job are effectively communicated to them
- instructions are given clearly and accurately
- their grievances are dealt with
- promises made are kept
- *all* safety regulations are kept
- infringements of safety regulations (written or not) are disciplined

 - everyone is treated alike
 - effective training programmes are arranged to improve their
   skills.

Meetings and reports

Meetings are endemic in organisational life. They serve a number of functions – they can serve to exchange information, discuss difficulties and explore alternative solutions. These are the tasks of meetings but of equal importance is the social aspect of meetings where they may be used as an integrating device to bring people together with a purpose of building commitment to the other people involved in the meeting. The production sub-system will use meetings to undertake some or all of the following activities:

1   Information gathering and sharing

Here the parties involved in the project may wish to meet to gather or share information. Issues such as the contractual commitments expected of the parties may need discussion in order to clarify understanding. Equally design and production details may be clarified at the meetings so that all parties are working from a common understanding of the project information. Obviously design changes may need to be discussed to explore the implications of any change upon the project as a whole.

2   Monitoring and control

Meetings can be used to monitor and control the works on site. Such meetings will be used to review progress, cost and quality standards against the targets established at the beginning of the project. Not only should meetings review any divergence from the plan but should discuss the various courses of action necessary to correct the situation. In such circumstances the meeting will be required to identify problems and explore solutions with all of the parties affected. Obviously there will be some points which are exclusive to one of the parties, for example the contractor may wish to meet separately to review costs performance as this may be seen as sensitive information.

3   Co-ordination

Meetings have a co-ordinating function. Frequently the work of a meeting is to co-ordinate sub-contractors and suppliers with the work of the main contractor. In management type contracts the management contractor or construction management contractor will be required to dedicate considerable effort into the co-ordination of sub or trade contractors and this will require frequent meetings to undertake this work. Such meetings could discuss issues such as timing of arrival of supplies or sub-contractors labour, facilities to be provided, procedures of labour relations, working methods, safety, bonusing, etc.

4 Problem solving meetings

Such meetings are frequently based upon task forces to solve particular problems besetting the project. These may fall within the other functions of meetings and most frequently problem solving meetings address issues such as delays, material shortage, labour problems, quality control, etc.

Reports

Another instrument for monitoring events on projects is the 'report'. Within the production sub-system reports are most frequently used to give feedback on progress or cost performance. In order to be effective reports need to be concise and follow a structure. The structure is usually as follows:

Executive summary	– A summary of the purpose and findings of the report. This should be limited to one page.
Introduction	– This will explain the purpose of the report and its theme, eg Quality control of the concrete in retaining walls on site.
Main report	– This will explore the theme of the report and collect and present data and evidence. It will seek to explore reasons for the events which led to the report, eg the reasons for poor quality on the retaining walls is . . .
Conclusions and Recommendations	– This summarises the findings of the report, and makes recommendations for any changes in practice which are necessary. No new information should be introduced into the conclusions.

6.4   Outputs

As seen in figure 6.1 the outputs are divided into two. To recap they are:

Tangible production which would be the production which has been dedicated to make the building grow

Intangibles which are the issues which flow from the production sub-system.

These outputs are issues such as the experience gained by the parties to the project which in turn would influence their capacity to undertake similar projects in the future. This improves the market intelligence within the firm. Also the level of satisfaction gained from doing the project and the level of satisfaction experienced by the users of the new building will also be an important yet intangible output of the production sub-system. Figure 6.5 shows the issues which will be useful in analysing the outputs of the production sub-system.

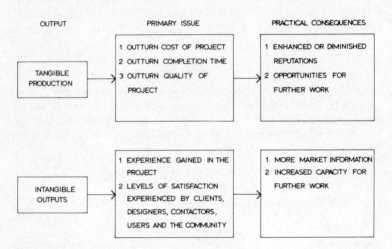

6.5 The outputs of the production system

Tangible production

The primary issues
Outturn costs will have different meanings to different parties in the contract. To the contractor who is operating in a traditional contract the importance of outturn cost is related to the profitability of the contract. Costs are related to the expenditure made to complete the project and are hopefully less than payments made by the client for the work.

To the client the outturn costs will be what she/he has had to pay for the building and comparisons with what the anticipated cost was and the outturn cost may be a significant measure of client satisfaction.

It is not intended to discuss the mechanics of cost control systems in this chapter but merely highlight the importance of delivering the project at the anticipated costs.

Outturn cost to the contractor
In a traditional contract the difference between the tendered amount and any extra payments and the costs experienced by the

contractor is likely to shape perceptions of how satisfactory the project was from the contractors' point of view.

At the outset of a project, indeed in the pre-contract stage there will usually be a plan of how the project is to be financially controlled. This plan may be formulated in a number of ways; the provision of budgets for major elements of the work is common as this links with the way that the Bill of Quantities is usually prepared and priced. However alternatives are available in using the network submitted as part of the contract documents to control time as well as costs. Each activity in the network can be allocated a budget and costs controlled in conjunction with time as work in the activity proceeds. Whichever system is chosen periodic monitoring is essential so that timely corrective action can be taken. In order to monitor costs the site management team need to prepare or be provided with cost plans which relate to elemental and/or component breakdown and short term budgets. These then express themselves as cost plans and measurements for comparing actual expenditure with the planned costs. Finally interim payments need to be related to the value of work done and compared against the costs of producing the work.

In management or fee contracts the costs to the managing contractor are more defused. Most of the financial risk will lay with sub-contractors and the 'profitability' of the project is related to the percentage fee earned. When Guaranteed Maximum Prices are quoted to clients and this figure is broached, can the managing contractor suffer financial loss.

Outturn cost – to the client
Not only will contractors be interested in what the project has cost them to build but the client will be interested in any differences in what he expected to pay for the building at the outset and the amount paid in the final account. It is where severe escalations are experienced that the image of the construction industry is tainted. Increasingly clients have been recommended to become more involved in monitoring project costs. Yet in many traditional contracts the architect acts as a surrogate client and contractors only know client expectations (in respect of costs) second hand. However, the authority of the client has been evolving during this century from a naive individual to a sophisticated corporate organisation. Figure 6.6 depicts this progression.

This change in types of clients has been matched with an increasing number of options in terms of methods of payment for work and contracts under which the work can be carried out. As ROWLINSON (1988) points out 'the building client has to make some choice over the way (financial) risks in the building process are to be shared. The client can influence the distribution of risk by his choice of payment method and his approach to selecting his design and construction organisation'. ROWLINSON (op cit) goes on to depict the risk associated with payment and section methods in two diagrams.

This concept of risk sharing has been expressed in the way contractors have agreed to offer clients guaranteed maximum price contracts. The key selling point is that the contractor undertakes to give the client a share of any saving if he completes the work below an agreed price. This offers the client some certainties regarding outcome costs and stimulates contractors to seek to reduce the construction costs.

Outturn completion time
Timely completion of a project is frequently seen as a major criteria of project success. Yet despite this shibboleth there has been almost universal criticism of failures of the building industry to deliver projects in a timely way. This problem has been well

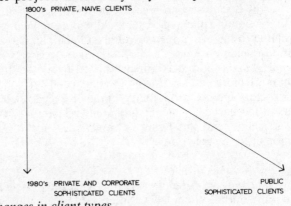

6.6   Changes in client types

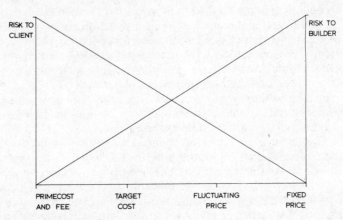

6.7   Risk and payment method

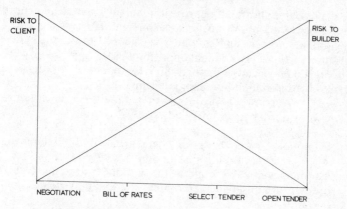

6.8   Risk and selection method

documented since the 1960s, BROMILOW (1974) working in Australia studied 370 building projects and found that contracts overran on average a staggering 47% over the original time budget. In Britain, WOOD (1975), observed that on a sample of over 2000 projects the average time overrun was 17% with some 1200 projects over-running by 5% and 600 projects by over 20% of the planned time.

This search for greater certainty in terms of time needs to be set against the background of performance of the industry in the mid-1970s. Concern about performance led GRAVES (1978) to survey the satisfaction of industrial clients. He reported that 17% of the sample were dissatisfied by the time taken to complete their project. Also reviewing industrial buildings MOBBS (1976) compared the performance of the building industry in several countries and claimed that the UK building industry took 70% longer to delivery buildings than other countries. Finally the NEDO report *Faster Building for Industry* (1983) surveyed the time taken for industrial projects and it questioned whether traditional contractual arrangements were providing clients with buildings in the shortest possible time. It recommended the greater use of management methods used in the USA and such procedures are increasingly used in European construction settings.

These 'fast-track' methods have become increasingly popular in reducing the overall project duration.

This approach was recommended by the *Faster Building for Industry* report (op cit) which studied the speed of construction projects and the research concluded that there was 'substantial scope for improving the general pace of construction of industrial building without sacrificing quality or increasing costs'. The argument presented was that a project success was a function of management effort necessary to complete on time and this disciplined approach helped to control costs and quality. Furthermore the research showed that projects planned to a 'safe' and more leisurely targets ultimately do not finish on time. This was supported by a number of case studies which considered the construction programmes – these showed that opportunities for time saving were not being taken because opportunites for parallel working was restricted by the availability of supervision.

In order to achieve a project with a timely outturn, *Faster Building for Industry* recommended:

  – customers with knowledge of what is achievable and requiring a short time, accurately specified by dates or deadlines
  – customers well advised about the workings of the method of contract organisation and about the building team they choose
  – coherent management responsibility for the progress of the project throughout
  – overlapping pre-construction activities
  – project arrangements which allow early, precise and integrated procurement and preparation for construction
  – a clear statement of design which takes into account practical aspects of organising work on site
  – competent and adequate site management and supervision
  – control over site labour resources
  – good communications and incentive to complete on time.

Outturn quality

As clients become more demanding and price become less sensitive when contracts are let then the quality of the product assumes a greater significance when judging client satisfaction. Traditionally the construction industry relied upon quality control procedures to ensure the quality of the completed building. More recently Quality Assurance has emerged as a mechanism by which clients can be satisfied that they are receiving a reliable, high-quality building.

It is useful to distinguish the two different aspects of obtaining quality within the production sub-system. Quality control is primarily a system of checking that a product introduced into the building meets specific requirements. These may be measurable in terms of a weight, dimensions, strength etc set down by a particular British Standard. Most components in building are covered by a British Standard and these standards will define the boundaries of imperfections. Any materials falling outside these boundaries are not acceptable and the function of quality control is to isolate these rogue components, eg bricks too big or too small, concrete too wet, etc. But each building will have its own quality standards which are set by the specification. This will define the quality boundaries for the particular project by defining tolerances and standards expected for each element of the work. Having recognised these established

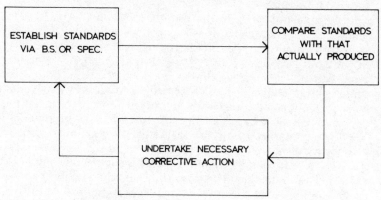

6.9   Control loops

standards the site management team have a bench mark against which to control quality on site. To present it in the classical control loop the quality control function may be shown as a circular diagram as shown in figure 6.9.

Quality Assurance on the other hand focuses upon consumer protection and offers clients an *assurance* that the building has been built properly under satisfactory conditions of quality control and that the building has been judged suitable for its intended use. In short quality assurance is giving clients guarantees that the building will continue to perform as required for a reasonable period of time. This differs from quality control which is a process which focuses upon the identification of defects during construction.

During the late 1980s several construction organisations sought to ensure the outturn quality by seeking certification with the British Standards Institute for quality assured processes undertaken by their firms. Practices and contractors had applied to the BSI for Quality Assurance (QA) registration under BS 5750. In short quality assurance certification was given if firms could demonstrate that they:

- planned the services they gave to clients
- did what they planned
- documented what was done.

To many this is merely a statement of good practice but pressure for certification may begin to be exerted by clients and insurers. Moreover in heightened competition it is likely that those firms not certified will be seen to be providing an inferior service. This obviously has implications for the marketing of services provided by construction organisations.

Intangible outputs

The tangible outcomes of the project will lead to enhanced or diminished reputation of the participants. Increasingly reputation is seen as a commodity which has commercial value and building organisations which have fostered and developed a good reputation can frequently command a premium price for their work. The primary production activities of the system are the key to developing a reputation and completion on time, within budget and to the appropriate quality standards all enhance a company's reputation. Yet this reputation has to be marketed; it is of little value if prospective clients are not aware that a company is noted for all of these positive attributes. Therefore one of the intangible outputs of the production sub-system must be a mechanism of public relations which tells the world how good a firm is at performing the principal tasks of construction. Coverage in journals or local newspapers of fast building, under budget completions, skilful handling of difficult and hazardous site conditions, etc, can be used as promotional material for the firm with consequent enhancement of reputation.

At a more fundamental level the enhancement of reputation may be sustained by the visible signs of the site – clean walkways, good hoardings with spy-holes if appropriate, clean and tidy sites which operate in a safe way can do most to present the firm in a positive way. In addition a 'good neighbour' policy with building users around the site can build reputations. It is these facets of the production sub-system which are the product of good production management on site.

At another level the process of doing the project will add to the participant's stock of experience which will shape the amount of market information that the participants have. In a practical sense this can assist contractors in identifying particular market niches in which they have expertise and experience. This may be as broad as say civil engineering construction or a niche within this large market, say road building. Another type of niche may be geographical or by client type.

Clearly information about production performance will need to be held within the information sub-system as this will shape how the contractor is to behave in the event of being invited to tender for similar projects in the future. Thus the production sub-system is linked to the information sub-system as a provider of market intelligence. For example the production sub-system will need information about sub-contractors in a particular area of a new project. The information sub-system should enable an interrogation for the production system to obtain this information.

Doing projects well also offers the prospect of enjoying the vision of that rare beast – the satisfied client. NAOUM (1988) tested the level of satisfaction experienced by clients on 39 management contracts and 30 traditional contracts. On each project he asked clients to express their level of satisfaction with the project outcome in terms of the three dimensions of project success, time, cost and quality. NAOUM (op cit) found that clients using the management contracting system expressed high satisfaction (in respect to time) in greater numbers than the clients using traditional procurement methods. Table 6.1 shows the research result.

Level of satisfaction	Management contracting clients	Traditional system clients
High	79%	52%
Moderate	13%	28%
Low	8%	20%

Table 6.1   Procurement method and client satisfaction in respect of time

The contrast between the systems is less marked when cost is considered. Here there is no significant difference between the expressed level of satisfaction as table 6.2 shows.

Level of satisfaction	Management contracting clients	Traditional system clients
High	55%	53%
Moderate	26	28
Low	19	18

Table 6.2   Procurement method and client satisfaction in respect of cost

Finally client assessments of their satisfaction in respect of quality was compared. It was recognised that quality is a highly subjective matter and difficult to compare since there is no objective yardstick such as a budget or project programme. Overall NAOUM found little difference in the levels of satisfaction experienced in the two systems as table 6.3 shows. It must be noted that levels of satisfaction with quality seem to be unusually high.

Level of satisfaction	Management contracting clients	Traditional system clients
High	65%	72%
Moderate	24	20
Low	11	8

Table 6.3   Procurement method and client satisfaction in respect of quality

Whilst client satisfaction is probably the most important criteria in an industry becoming more market orientated, other parties must also be considered. Designers will wish to find satisfaction in being able to express their creativity through the building as a product whilst users will need to feel that the building 'works' for them.

The community will need to be assured that new buildings fit into the context of adjacent buildings. These aspects of user and community satisfaction are linked to designer satisfaction; designers need to build their reputation by producing buildings which are welcomed by the public but also satisfy the users. It is a difficult equation to solve.

Finally, contractors will need to find a level of satisfaction in the project. Unlike other parties involved the contractor may find more satisfaction in the process of the construction rather than the finished product. The axiom of 'a good job to work on' is an oft used expression of satisfaction. These expressions speak of the quality of relationships on the project much more than the finished product. A cruder, but nonetheless important, measure is the profitability of the contract for the builder. Similar considerations will apply to subcontractors on the project.

These 'soft' issues have strong business implications for the builder. By undertaking projects they gain more experience and this provides the builder with improved market information with an improved capacity for further work by developing a track record in completed projects. In an industry which is moving towards a market rather than a production orientation it is vital that potential clients perceive these skills and experience.

6.5   Feedback (monitoring)

A part of the systems model which was used to drive this chapter (figure 6.1) showed that the outputs had to be monitored to ensure that correction can be made to the input during the life of a project or for the benefit of the next project. The inputs will bring together a project plan which sets out the resource needs. This plan can control the work but will require continuous monitoring to measure the plan against actual achievements. This monitoring component of the production system needs to identify deviations from the plan and so shape management decisions to take advantage of beneficial trends or undertake corrective action. The information sub-system within the organisation will be connected to the feedback activity. The feedback aspect of the production sub-system can be represented as in figure 6.10.

But not only will the feedback need to be obtained it is important that it is fed to the appropriate level for action. Different levels of management within the building organisation will require different

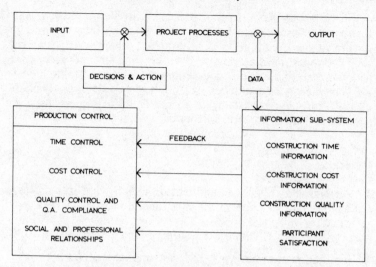

6.10   Feedback loops in the production system

presentations of the same information. Directors will require an overview of progress whilst rate supervisors will need specific and detailed information concerning progress of particular trades and sub-contractors. This can be presented in a diagram as shown in figure 6.11.

As projects become longer and more complex, clients become more demanding, there is a greater need for more formal methods

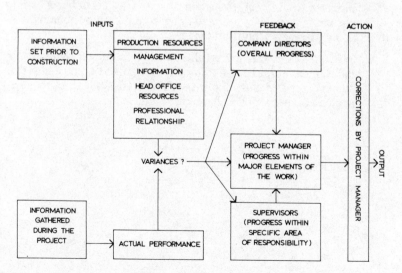

6.11   Information needs of project participants

of providing feedback so that projects may be monitored. Such feedback loops need to be integrated into the information sub-system of the organisation (see Volume 1 chapter 5). However, such feedback mechanisms need to be built around procedures which are not inflexible and an end in themselves. People have to use such mechanisms of feedback and they should positively not be used as an instrument to allocate blame. They are properly used in a spirit of collective problem solving not retribution.

Questions

1 Analyse the technical and social factors that determine a builder's production strategy in the construction of a new building.

CIOB Part II *Building Management* Paper II 1987

2 Interaction between line and staff management may have a significant effect upon the efficiency of the production system in building firms.
 (a) Discuss how this interaction may be achieved.
 (b) Outline the barriers (between line and staff) which may need to be overcome.

3 Identify and discuss the duties of a site manager working on:
 (i) a traditional site
 (ii) a management contract site
 (iii) a construction management site.
 In cases (ii) and (iii) the site manager may be defined as the person in charge of the managing contracting or construction management activities on the site.

4 Site management responsibility must be to deliver buildings to the client as it was specified, within the agreed budget and in the allowed time. Assess the inputs required and the processes needed to be carried out to achieve these tasks.

7 Marketing the Outputs

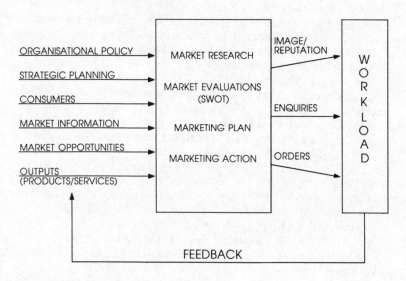

7.1 *The marketing system*

7.1 Primary Task

The Primary Task is:

> To ensure that the organisation secures the most suitable work, produces the best outputs and sells those outputs in the most appropriate ways.

7.2 Introduction

Frequently, marketing is confused with selling. Although on occasions the terms are used interchangeably, the two activities are quite different. Selling is a separate process but one which is part of the total marketing activity.

The Institute of Marketing (1973) defined marketing as:

> 'The management function which organises and directs all those business activities involved in assessing and converting purchasing power into effective demand for a specific product or service

and in moving the product or service to the final customer so as to achieve the profit target or other objectives set by a company.'

LEVITT (1968) described selling as focusing 'on the needs of the seller. . . . Selling is preoccupied with the seller's needs to convert his product into cash'.

Thus, the essence of selling is persuading potential customers to acquire the organisation's outputs; to create an outflow of products (or services) from the organisation and a consequent inflow of cash to it. Selling may occur directly to final consumers/customers, eg sale of a speculatively built house, or indirectly via intermediaries such as agents, eg bricks, retailers, eg taps, or to producers of final products/services, eg sale of precast concrete components to a contractor. Selling takes place through personal contact, eg visits by sales representatives, or by impersonal media, eg sales catalogues.

Marketing involves matching an organisation's resources with the wants of consumers; as such marketing comprises analysis, planning and control activities. The consumers' wants must be in the form of effective demand (desire supported by purchasing power) for those consumers to constitute actual or potential customers of the organisation. Matching is achieved through the use of a 'Marketing Mix' – the four Ps – **Product**, **Price**, **Promotion** and **Place**.

The marketing sub-system is illustrated in figure 7.1. Inputs comprise the organisation's policy and its strategy planning, consumers are inputs as the sub-system seeks to convert them into potential customers (making enquiries) and then actual customers (placing orders). Both information about and opportunities in the organisation's markets are required and will relate to the markets in which the organisation operates and those within which it could work. The final input to the marketing sub-system is the organisation's outputs – the products and/or services which the organisation produces, how they are produced and their attributes (probably evaluated in terms of time, cost and quality aspects).

The sub-system's conversion process includes market research, evaluations, planning and action. Research is used to glean data and information relating to the markets which are then subjected to measurements and judgments in the context of the organisation's goals. Subsequently plans are formulated and actions taken towards the realisation of those plans. The outputs resulting from marketing processes are the image and reputation of the organisation, enquiries inviting the organisation to seek work (usually by a procedure involving limited/selective competition; traditionally with price being the major variable but with time and quality playing increasingly important roles) and the securing of orders for the organisation to execute work.

The outcome of the marketing sub-system is the organisation's workload – mix and quantity. Feedback is vital to the sub-system, especially as input variables and the environmental circumstances may change quite rapidly, to enable the marketing activities to keep abreast of current developments and expectations of the future.

BELL (1981) found that marketing was in its infancy amongst construction organisations; more specifically, that it was common for contractors to treat marketing as a distinct and separate business function. The result of that situation is that construction organisations' marketing has tended to be reactive rather than proactive, ie organisations respond to changes which have occurred in the market rather than discover indications, predict changes and adapt accordingly. Such an approach is a further facet of the conservative nature of the industry.

One additional problem is the nature of the construction industry – whether it is a production or a service industry. In the UK, the Standard Industrial Classification notes construction to be a service industry. The distinction is of importance as it indicates what is to be marketed – the buildings themselves or the (service of the) provision of the buildings. Increasingly construction organisations are concerned with the processes of building provisions; most main contractors sub-let the vast majority of construction work and so, effectively, are management contractors whatever procurement system is used nominally. Design certainly is a service and it appears that only in the provision of materials, goods and components are products obtained.

7.3 Inputs

Organisational policy

An organisation's policy is constrained by the areas and objectives of operation set out in fundamental documents used to set-up the organisation, eg partnership agreement; articles of association and memorandum of association of a company. However, such documents usually are worded in such broad terms that they seldom impose any significant restrictions. Hence organisations can carry out a variety of activities in most market sectors.

Possibly of greater significance is the ethos of the organisation, frequently manifested by the organisational form adopted. Organisational forms such as friendly societies and co-operatives seldom operate in the same profit seeking fashion as do most companies, partnerships, etc; they operate on a 'social conscience' basis. So although building co-operatives may seek profits, they also may undertake work at cost for poorer members of the society, eg pensioners.

Other facets of organisation's policies may preclude their undertaking work for certain clients, eg clients linked with the tobacco industry or with South African connections. Other policies may restrict marketing activities, notably forms of promotion used and media for advertising. A common policy amongst construction contractors is not to tender for work in open competition due to the costs involved and the perceived chances of submitting a successful bid.

Strategic planning
Within the context of organisational policy, strategic planning denotes directions and goals to be achieved. Of particular interest to the marketing sub-system are the plans relating to turnover, in both magnitude and composition, and those relating to price and non-price competitive actions. Especially if entry into a new market sector is planned, an essential consideration will be whether, and to what extent, any internal subsidies will be provided to ease entry by allowing prices to be kept at a low level (relative to market prices in that new sector) until the organisation has become established. Special promotions budgets for such diversifications are likely to be necessary.

Thus, the strategic planning components of marketing concern determinations of what to produce and how to move the outputs to customers to meet the organisation's goals, ie in which industry(s) to operate and in which market(s). For entry into new areas of production/markets the attractions (profitability, etc) must be sufficient but it is important that the evaluations do take into account the full costs of entry – set up costs, promotional programmes, initial subsidies, etc.

Strategic planning should consider gains which may accrue through acquisition of market dominance. Such may be achieved through size to enable the organisation to be a price leader in a situation of price (and non-price) competition or by its acquiring a sole right to produce, such as by obtaining a patent on a product. The former may occur through growth, however achieved, whilst the latter results from research and development activities.

Consumers
Everyone consumes the outputs of the construction industry either directly or indirectly. However, not everyone is either an actual or potential customer of the industry as customers exercise demand. Marketing seeks maximisation of customers from a set of consumers but, perhaps more particularly, to secure the greatest number of actual customers from the potential customers.

Customers of the construction industry comprise individuals (purchasing new houses), local authorities (purchasing schools, etc), other public sector bodies (purchasing airports, hospitals, roads, etc) and private sector organisations – notably industry and commerce (purchasing factories, offices, etc). With the exception of speculative developments, it is usual for the construction organisation to have sold its output before the output is produced (applies to both design and construction through the bidding/tendering procedures).

Speculative developments are most common in private sector housing, offices and in industrial construction. Particularly in major urban centres, developers are involved in refurbishments of commercial premises as well as the provision of new buildings. The marketing activities of speculative developers determine the location, type timing and extent of their construction. Especially in housing, the developer tends to be the builder also although it is normal for the construction operations to be sub-contracted; glossy publicity, advertising, a site sales office and a show house are features of most larger housing developments. Developers aim to have sales as early as possible (frequently, houses are sold before construction of those actual units has begun) to ensure certainty of sales (not a common problem) and cash inflow. In speculative housing developments the sales rate is used to determine the required pace of production and completions schedule.

Speculative developers of commercial and industrial premises usually avoid the large land banks of housing developers. These (former) organisations may be part of a construction group and/or linked to a property company (which will acquire and operate a development on its completion; alternatively, the development will be sold to a separate property company or, occasionally, a final user, the latter being more common for industrial developments).

Property development processes are described in texts such as SEELEY (1983), HARVEY (1987) and FRASER (1984).

As much construction is sold prior to the work's being done, the marketing concerns an abstract product or service. The conversion of consumers into customers concerns convincing them that they require a building, or building work, whilst the conversion of potential customers into actual ones necessitates the customers' being convinced that the building needs are met best by the particular construction organisation concerned.

Particularly for contractors operating under the traditional procurement system, part of their marketing must be directed at consultants (architects, quantity surveyors, etc) as those parties are very influential over clients in determining which contractors are invited to bid and, ultimately, to which contractor a project is awarded. So consultants act as a type of intermediate customer; indeed they execute some marketing on behalf of contractors. Equally, to some degree, consultant's marketing relies on contractors (and other consultants) through the use of complete projects to demonstrate abilities and expertise in the securing of new commissions.

Thus, a vital question for construction organisation's marketing is, 'Who is the buyer?', ie who is the party with greatest influence over whether the project is executed and, if so, by which organisation(s). The spectrum of parties with influence spans from sub-contractors and suppliers, through contractors and consultants, local authorities and statutory bodies to clients, tenants (users), financiers (banks and institutional investors) and pressure groups, eg Victorian Society; Town and Country Planning Association; Transport 2000; The Freedom Association. The consideration gives rise to a supplementary question, 'What is the correct stage of the project at which to sell the product/service?'.

The focus of the who and when questions is on selling and so deals with customers rather than consumers and concerns the generation of enquiries and their conversion into orders. These are dealt with as outputs of the marketing system.

Market information

The input to the marketing sub-system of market information is an output of the organisation's information system. As noted above, the information sub-system gathers and processes data and information both of which must be geared to the generation of the information required, in this instance, to facilitate efficient marketing.

Marketing should aim to generate orders which are the most suitable for the organisation – at a simple level, the most profitable. The organisation will be concerned about potential orders – size, location, type, parties, procurement form and competition. Data and information pertaining to the national situation are of limited use as contractors tend to operate within a restricted locality – within fifty miles of head or branch office is common, hence regionalisation of many major companies. Often consultants are not so constrained. So although national data may help by providing a 'feel' for the market and trends, to be of real use disaggregated data are required.

Apart from the general data available in various Central Statistical Office (CSO) publications, eg Housing and Construction Statistics; Annual Abstract of Statistics, national information is available via Building Cost Information Service, eg Building Cost Index; Tender Prices Index; Market Conditions Index; Cost Studies. An addition to the array of general data and information regarding the construction market(s) is the Building Market Report – which provides statistics of orders, output, costs and prices including some regional information plus articles upon current issues. Despite such publications it is quite apparent that to obtain specific market information, a construction organisation must undertake research of its own (either itself or via consultants).

Marketing information obtained by construction organisations covers the categories of customers, projects and competitors; such information must be 'organisation specific' to be of real assistance to the marketing efforts. Customers should be categorised by purchasing behaviour which yields a form of market segmentation. Segments are, in effect, separate (sub-)markets and may require different marketing strategies and techniques. The segments themselves must be distinguishable from other market segments, eg 'executive' housing; starter homes, but are internally homogeneous, of sufficient size to merit attention and accessible to the organisation.

It is unusual for construction organisations to pursue 'aggressive' marketing policies, it is normal for them to respond to enquiries, etc., rather than to attempt to generate enquiries (and, hence orders) from potential customers. However, particularly following the initiative of Barratt Homes promotional campaigns of the late 1970s and early 1980s (until the 'collapse' of the timber-framed housing market in England), construction organisations, especially those involved in speculative developments (most notably housing), have taken marketing much more seriously and have undertaken higher profile promotional campaigns.

The result of the stance adopted by construction organisations is that only housing developers require detailed information about potential customers and their locations, demand types, etc, in order to select what to construct, when and where. The more usual approach to information about customers is for construction organisations to research potential clients on receipt of an initial enquiry for a project or when considering requesting a place on a 'tender list'; the information sought is financial primarily – to ensure that the client is able to pay for the project (in accordance with the likely contractual provisions).

Construction organisations' primary marketing information is project based. The project based marketing has two components, the general component whereby the organisation determines the types, sizes, locations, etc, of projects which it wishes to undertake and structures itself accordingly, and the particular component where the promotion/selling of the organisation pursues potential projects. Information for the general component considers sizes, growth trends, profitabilities, locations, etc, of markets and market sectors whilst information for the particular components considers what projects may be available, where, when, from whom (client and consultants), etc, within the 'general' framework. Information regarding particular project proposals is obtained from sources such as advertisements for tenderers in 'Building' and local authorities' planning registers. The information sources are scrutinised regularly and frequently and suitable potential projects are noted. Appropriate parties (client, architect, quantity surveyor) are then approached, often personally, to seek an invitation to tender or, preferably, to negotiate the project.

Information concerning competitors is vital; most models of contractors' bidding, eg FRIEDMAN (1956), GATES (1967), CARR (1982), use competitors as a primary variable. It is fortunate that the models do not require the actual identity and bidding performance data relating to the competitors, as such data are sometimes neglected by contractors despite its provision via standard tendering procedures. (*Note*: Code of Procedure for Single Stage Selective Tendering; and related codes produced by NJCBI – National Joint Council for the Building Industry.) As the vast majority of bidding (contractors and, now, consultants) situations place the competitors in contexts of oligopoly (see, for example, LIPSEY (1979) and as bidding success rate is a primary determinant of bidding costs and, thence, profitability?) it is rather surprising that some construction organisations give so little attention to obtaining data and information about their competitors – both actual and potential.

For those organisations which do seek information about their competitors, a considerable volume is available. Companies' accounts provide basic information about size, trends, etc, and may reveal moves to enter new markets, changes in pricing policies, etc. Feedback from tendering often notes which organisations bid and what the bids submitted were – such information is provided after the contract has been let and the lists do not indicate which organisation submitted which bid. Observation of new organisations entering the market, levels of activity and promotional campaigns provide further information.

Traditionally the focus has been upon price competition (as noted in bidding models) but recently emphasis has shifted to include quality and time performance; for some clients these latter criteria dominate price considerations, eg developers of city centre commercial properties. Increasingly contractors provide the service of construction management; pre-qualification interviews of key personnel are commonplace and so recruitment by vigorous 'head-hunting' of particular post-holders is quite common also. With a fairly mobile workforce, the 'Who now employs who?' question is valuable information about competitors.

However, despite policies and activities of employee retention (via visible career structure, etc), increasing protection of trade secrets (including bids) tending to make organisations more insular and keen to gain an advantage over rivals, the 'grapevine' still provides much information surprisingly rapidly and reliably. Good personal contacts are essential to produce the necessary network of what information can be obtained – how, when, from whom – either directly or indirectly. A major role of the grapevine is to indicate which organisations are bidding for a project, possibly how keenly and usually, after the bidding has closed, what the bids were.

Market opportunities

Market opportunities represent possibilities for the organisation to gain, such as by converting consumers into customers, by converting potential customers into actual customers, by obtaining some advantage over competitors or by entering a new sphere of (profitable) activity. Market opportunities themselves are passive but their realisation requires action by the organisation. To merit action, the opportunity must be sufficiently attractive (in the contexts of anticipated outcome contributing towards the organisations' objectives) – most usually in terms of anticipated profit (or financial return). Thus, many contractors, even during periods of quite depressed workloads, consider project opportunities via open tendering to be insufficiently attractive to warrant action, ie no tendering action is taken, particularly due to the likely number of bidders and the resultant low profitability of the particular organisation obtaining the contract, the expected profitability does not merit the resources required (cost) to produce and submit a bid.[1]

That contractors' marketing has been found to be reactive rather than pro-active – BELL (1981) – is likely to be a reflection of the techniques employed. Traditionally, much marketing effort has been quite 'hidden' and 'unofficial' through the use of informal, even apparently casual, meetings as epitomised by the 'golf club contacts'. That mechanism for generating enquiries and some direct orders, operates through networks of personal contacts of people high in the management structure of the organisation – director or partner level. Such personal encounters are used to enhance potential clients' and consultants' awareness of the organisation's activities and expertise. The meetings are low key and seek to ensure that the organisation will be considered (favourably) when parties are invited to bid for work on new projects. Therefore concentration is upon potential clients who are known to be about to embark upon a project whilst meetings with others are used to maintain general awareness of the organisation.

Perhaps as a result of the prolonged recessionary period of the 1970s and early 1980s, construction organisations have adopted both more extensive and more proactive marketing. Changes in the operational environment of consultants through the instigation of fee competition, the increasing involvement of overseas based consultants and increased use of non-traditional procurement forms (project management, management contracting, design and build, etc,) has prompted many consultant practices to become more market orientated and to undertake extensive marketing activities.

To achieve a sale, WILSON (1972) suggests that a buyer must agree that:

---

[1] For further explanation – the grounds for the action and statistical basis – see, for example, MOORE (1980), FELLOWS *et al.* (1983).

1 A need exists
2 The service (product) offered is the correct one to meet the need
3 The organisation is able to provide the service (product)
4 The price is acceptable
5 The delivery time is satisfactory.

Combination of 1 and 2, given adequate financial resources of the buyer, results in demand – the market opportunity; addition of 3 (with expectations of 4 and 5) yields an enquiry and the combination of all five aspects produces an order.

Thus, market opportunities exist in two varieties – those which arise externally to the organisation and are manifested as enquiries/ orders, and those which are realised by the organisation's marketing, ie without the marketing, although the opportunity would exist, it would not be expressed to the organisation as an enquiry/ order.

Outputs

Construction organisations produce, market and sell outputs. The outputs are tangible, in the forms of products, components and finished buildings, and are intangible, in the form of services (design, management, assembly, etc) which contribute to the provision of the building.

Marketing concerns fostering awareness by customers of the outputs and/or their attributes together with what changes can be made to them and at what costs (quality and time as well as money). The counterpart also applies through making suppliers aware of customers' requirements (present and future) in order that the suppliers can respond by providing more suitable outputs.

Many changes in construction outputs have been, and are, client driven (such as the reductions in project durations and the emphasis on quality provision and quality assurance). Other changes are supplier driven, eg management contracting; timber framed housing.

As construction organisations operate in competitive environments, consideration must be given to the outputs of competitors as well as the particular organisation. Such consideration will comprise comparative evaluations to denote the output strengths, to which marketing/promotional/selling efforts can be devoted, and the weaknesses in the outputs which merit internal action for their rectification, ie output development effort.

As most outputs are bespoke ('one-offs') and even on apparently repetitive projects, eg housing estates, each unit has certain unique features, a significant problem is output control. The problem is exacerbated by factors such as environmental (weather, etc) variables, alterations to constituent components, eg colour of bricks, and, perhaps most especially, by movements of personnel between projects and organisations – operatives, designers and managers. The stability of a production line is not enjoyed in construction where, utlimately, performance is determined by the people at the site.

It is usual for output to be judged in terms of cost, time required and quality. Due to the potential impossibility of defining quality and, therefore, of measuring it, attributes of a project which are believed to contribute to its quality are evaluated, eg appearance; fitness for purpose. Marketing must take all three facets into account but the ultimate selling activity (usually conversion of an enquiry into an order via bidding) tends to be totally cost oriented with project duration and 'quality' being specified. Bidding for design, although largely cost oriented, usually encourages consideration of the quality of the finished building and often of the design consultants' inputs also; times for both design and construction will be variables at this stage. Similar situations are common where contractors seek involvement with non traditional methods of building procurement – usually involvement during design production to provide, inter alia, a buildability input to design.

A final aspect is that building proposals, ie models of construction outputs, increasingly are being evaluated on a life cycle basis rather than just the provision of the output and what the output is once produced. The problem with such evaluations is lack of data and paucity of the few data which are available.

Client requirements of and evaluation methods for outputs must form the basis which both the production and marketing sub-systems use when considering outputs.

7.4 Conversion process

Market research
Market research is concerned with gathering data and information about the organisation's current and potential markets; thus it bears much resemblance to the information sub-system. Where data and information are available, eg from Government bodies; trade associations, the activity comprises gathering, summarising, communicating, etc. Other data must be collected 'first hand', eg from planning registers; clients' financial situations. Whatever techniques are adopted, the research must produce the information in forms suitable for the market evaluations to be carried out; the overall context of the research, and hence the markets and sections investigated, will be determined by the organisation's policy and its strategic plan.

Market research, as an information providing activity, operates in three modes:

1   provision of information at regular intervals
2   investigation of the market in response to requests from production, sales, etc
3   occasional investigations of the market, particularly seeking potential opportunities and problems (threats).

The first mode is the basic reactive mode. It includes investigation of published data and information which relates to the organisation's market environment plus obtaining information about potential projects to facilitate the organisation's achieving production/sales targets (often expressed as turnover). The information from such research is provided for evaluation at regular intervals and is collected in a cyclic way – governed by publication dates and circuits of regular visits to local authorities' planning departments, etc.

The second mode comprises ad hoc investigations instigated by sections of the organisation which have detected the (possible) onset of problems or opportunities; again the research is reactive. The third mode is pro-active. If it is not present in the research mix, progress in the market is likely to be 'stumbling'.

Often research is instigated with the detection that a 'problem' may exist, proceeds through defining and investigating the problem and concludes with production and evaluation of possible solutions and recommending a course of action which appears to be the best one to follow. The technique employed in market research include desk research (study of publications) and empirical (field work, eg questionnaire of clients' building needs), ad hoc or one-off studies of particular issues to continuously monitoring markets, reactive to the organisations' problems, etc, to pro-active (market 'creation' via vigorous promotions) and investigations of factors (variables) both internal and external to the organisation.

A good market intelligence sub-system is a product of good market researching. Data, passive 'facts and figures', are used to produce information – active data with directions; analyses yield intelligence which is required for decisions and, thence, planning. (*For example*: data – 5 billion bricks were sold during 1987; information – 3.5 billion of those bricks were produced by company 'X'; intelligence – reasons for the size of the market and the position occupied by 'X', eg purchasers' preferences; price; delivery. The intelligence would assist another brick producer in deciding how to improve its market share.)

It is important to remember that market information/intelligence is perishable. Market situations may change rapidly, eg tendering opportunity for a project, so the organisation must be able to respond with sufficient speed. As most construction outputs are occasioned through derived demand (they are producers/investment goods), research must pay attention to the 'root' demands being the final products and services. The accelerator effect applies with varying leads for the different construction outputs and sectors and these must be taken into account when forecasting demand for construction; this aspect is particularly important in assisting organisations in smoothing peaks and troughs in workloads.

WILSON (1972) believes that market research, for a service organisation, should seek answers to the following questions:

Is a service needed?
What service is needed?
Who needs the service?
How should the service be rendered?
Who should render the service?

The answers should attempt to identify the characteristics of regular, occasional and discontinued clients, non-clients due to quotations which have failed (rejected tender) and those due to the non-receipt of an enquiry (no invitation to tender), and other potential clients in the market. Naturally, characteristics of competitors (both actual and potential) are important as is the view taken of the nature of market competition, eg oligopoly, contestable markets – BUTTON (1985).

BELL (1981) concluded that investigating Government expenditure plans, local authorities' planning registers, etc, provides an organisation with only rough guidance about future markets but that it is vital to research existing and new jobs and market sectors, which produces specific market intelligence.

Once customers have been found, research must discover the decision making units of those customers and the people concerned. Those people determine whether, how, when, to whom, etc, an order will be given. Most clients of the industry are complex organisations in which committees and/or hierarchies (rather than individuals) make decisions about placing contracts. CHERNS and BRYANT (1984) showed that when clients' decisions about building projects reach the construction industry, they are the results of resolutions of internal 'struggles' of the client. It is of much help if market research reveals the 'enthusiasts' and the 'antis' in the client's decision making units, the natures of those people, etc, as they will merit the use of different marketing approaches and emphasis on different aspects in the selling process.

People have selective perceptions – customers pay attention only to those facets of the service or goods which they believe to be important (price, styling, delivery time, etc). Research should aim to reveal customers' criteria for choice, often classified as functional criteria (physical properties of the outputs) and non-functional criteria (appearance, etc). However, from the viewpoint of effecting sales it is important to discover those attributes of the output which are qualifiers (analogous to HERTZBERG's hygiene factors in that they are assumed to be present and, if not or if inadequate will ruin the organisations' chances of further sales, eg compliance with quality statements/requirements), and those which are 'winners' (analogous to 'motivators' in that they distinguish the output and put it at an advantage to secure sales, eg reduced construction times; low tender sums). Qualifiers yield an enquiry but winners produce the order. Naturally winners, if reversed, eg high price, equally can be losers; qualifiers, if presumed by customers to be present but found not to be so, eg inadequate performance/quality, will be losers of subsequent potential enquiries and orders.

Market evaluations

The results of market research are used for market evaluations. The evaluations examine what the organisation does/could produce and what the market requires/will require. A common approach is SWOT analysis in which the Strengths and Weaknesses of the organisation are considered (internal factors) together with the Opportunities and Threats which the organisation faces (external factors). Evaluations necessitate placing the factors in order/ hierarchy, requiring that the factors have been measured by some means, if only subjective/intuitive and considering the results against the organisation's objectives so that the most advantageous results which are indicated can be the subjects of planned actions (marketing planning and marketing action).

Market evaluations will show what outputs are feasible for the organisation and what are beyond the organisation's abilities – areas of expertise are of particular relevance in the service sector of the economy. Although expertise can be acquired, it takes time and recruitment, education and training are expensive.

Evaluation is assisted by classification of the variables to facilitate planning of appropriate areas of action. Typically variables will be classified under market, product, producer, distributors, environment and relations (between parties).

The outcome of SWOT analyses leads an organisation to capitalise on its strengths through pursuing/creating market opportunities and to remove (or, at least, diminish) its weaknesses and act to avoid, overcome or remove external threats. It is common for threats to be identified as competitors, eg a large, well established organisation setting up in the locality, but it may be difficult to determine whether something is a threat or a weakness, eg clients requiring shorter construction periods than the organisation would provide usually. Research should provide the answer – if through comparative analyses other organisations can meet the required times, there is a weakness; if competitors are in a similar position, a threat exists. Likewise, strengths are relative also and so should be monitored and developed constantly to ensure their continuing relevance and existence.

Evaluations may begin with the market or the output. If market based, the matching will be of output to the attributes which the market requires; if output based, promotion, etc, will be of the output's particular strengths and the marketing function may need to create new markets to suit the output.

As outputs develop, such as in the product life cycle depicted in figure 7.2, so facets of the output may alter in nature (market perception/rquirements) between qualifiers and winners. Traditionally, construction time has been a qualifier and construction price (tender or bid) the winner. However, especially in commercial, city centre developments it is common for time to be the primary winner with price as a second winner; quality tends to remain a qualifier, although that an organisation is certified for quality assurance may prove to be a winner.

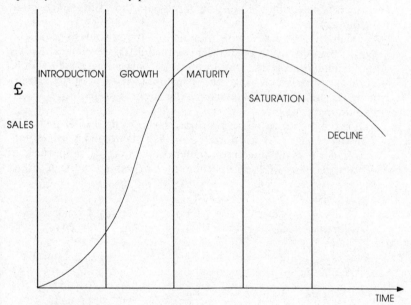

7.2   Product life cycle

Marketing plan

Following evaluations of the market alternatives, an organisation will produce a marketing plan. As plans must be 'forward-looking', it is unfortunate that construction organisations use rather few forecasting techniques; deterministic trend extrapolations combined with predictions based upon 'experience' and known factors, eg Government statements of future expenditure, are used but probability-based techniques are avoided.

For a plan to be effective, an essential ingredient is the

commitment to it of the organisation's personnel – it must be regarded as 'our plan', not 'your plan'. A good way of achieving identification with, and, hence, commitment to, the plan is by involving people in its production through consultations, discussions and agreement. Such an approach is important in construction which is a highly labour intensive industry and because true marketing includes production, promotion and sales processes.

All organisations are subject to resource constraints.

The constraints occur in terms of quantities, qualities and timing of resource availabilities, eg predicted finance available; organisation's personnel; project cash flows. Whatever evaluation methods have been employed, the evaluation should have produced a ranking of proposals – a form of hierarchy of items for inclusion in the marketing plan. Therefore an important aspect of the planning process is matching the most favourable proposals to the available resources.

From the basic planning method of survey-analysis-plan, the typical planning cycle, as shown in figure 7.3, has developed. Within the available proposals and applicable constraints, a plan should seek the employment of a fairly constant level of resources and to achieve any major changes in the resources required in an evolutionary manner.

It is helpful if the plan is produced giving individual attention to *Existing Markets*, *New Markets*, *Existing Outputs* and *New Outputs* as well as their combined requirements and effects. The approach is advantageous as different treatments are necessary for the different

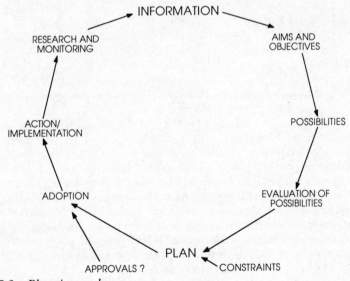

7.3 *Planning cycle*

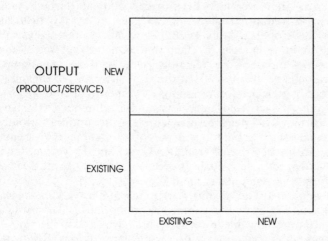

OUTPUT NEW
(PRODUCT/SERVICE)

EXISTING

EXISTING   NEW

7.4   Market matrix   MARKET

situations, shown in matrix format in figure 7.4. Further, the marketing plan must be compatible with the organisation's corporate plan.

An important facet of any plan is the assumptions which were used in its production. It is essential that the assumptions are stated clearly, possibly in an introduction or preamble to the plan, together with any assessments which have been made of the associated risks. The statements and risk assessments are helpful during the adoption process by indicating the expected consequences of implementing the plan. Often 'downside risks' are of special interest – these are the risks of the assumptions' not being fulfilled, ie the risks of shortfalls in the results of implementing the plan.

Organisations have different degrees of aversion to risk; those which are less risk averse will tend to be more 'adventurous' in their activities. Using figure 7.4, risks can be considered in terms of combinations of output types and market types, risks increasing from existing outputs in existing markets to new outputs in new markets. Allocation of risks (and uncertainties) between outputs and markets is helpful as organisations should have much control over their outputs but often precious little control over the markets.

The plan will set targets in relation to the four Ps of marketing – *Product*, *Price*, *Promotion* and *Place*, ie *the Marketing Mix*. The targets must be achievable, and identifiably so, by those who will be required to implement the plan (otherwise such people will be demoralised and demotivated by being given an apparently hopeless task).

On receipt of an enquiry by a construction organisation, *Product* and *Place* are prescribed – the project documents dictate what is to be constructed, its standard and where the project is to be located.

For developers, however, such decisions are theirs and so will form major elements of their marketing plans (see above – influences on decisions regarding land banking and timing of developments). Derived from the strategic plan, an organisation will decide in which locations/areas it wishes to operate and so the marketing plan will indicate what actions are intended to take place in particular localities. The plan will show the product attributes to be emphasised in promotions, ie the expected 'winners' – essentially these are process based (rapid construction to give time saving, ability to produce high quality buildings, etc); the plan also will note the form(s) promotions are to take.

Promotion occurs in different forms at the various stages of marketing. It is in the sphere of promotion that construction organisations have made considerable advances. Relaxations and changes in the regulations of professional institutions (RIBA, ICE, RICS etc) have allowed consultants to achieve much higher profiles in the construction market via advertising and participation in a much wider spectrum of activities, eg design and construction. Traditionally, construction organisations' promotions were by personal contacts with prospective clients and consultants (the 'golf-club' approach – still an important method), site sign boards and occasional newspaper advertisements; articles about success-ful, prestige projects featured in the trade press and professional journals. Now a full gamut of promotions often is employed – the traditional techniques are maintained but bolstered by major advertising in several media; sophisticated, glossy publicity brochures are common as are sponsorships of high profile events and advertising at television-covered events, eg football matches, thereby reaching a vast number of people.

Direct television advertising was pioneered by Barratt Ltd which undertook a nationwide campaign to promote its houses. Other housebuilders, eg Wimpey, soon followed but consequent upon the destruction of the public's confidence in timber framed housing (on which Barratt concentrated) and the resultant drastic decline in demand, television advertising has been curtailed.

Although *Price*, as contract (tender) sum is diminishing in importance, it remains the most common determinant of which (of the pre-selected) construction organisations executes the project. Thus the marketing plan must set pricing strategies. Naturally, the tactics may vary depending on the project, client, consultants, workload, etc, but the plan should set out the approaches to be taken. Frequently, turnover targets are set for the market sectors and bidding will occur accordingly – see figure 7.5. (Bidding is discussed under *Marketing action* page 135).

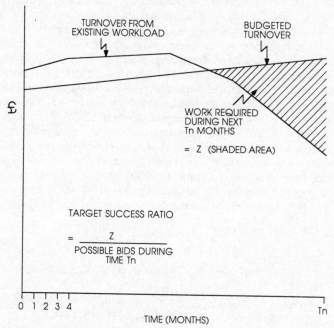

7.5 Turnover targetting

The marketing plan will denote how prices will be set – whether by the usual estimating and tendering techniques or/and by unorthodox methods such as cost plus a fee. For some time, Bovis Ltd adopted solely a cost plus fee pricing method and, coupled with cultivation of major, repeating clients, proved to be very successful.

Marketing action

Marketing action is the implementation of the marketing plan. Therefore, it includes promotion of the organisation and its outputs, obtaining orders and arranging production to yield the desired outputs. Achieving the outputs through production is considered in other chapters of this book.

Promotion of an organisation occurs on two levels – the creation of a general image/reputation and making representations to particular customers. The general image is the province of advertising whilst making representations is a personal process and is targetted to obtain an enquiry or/and an order. Representations range from the golf-club contacts to interviews of management teams for proposed projects.

Direct 'mail-shot' promotion is used extensively. To be effective, it must be targetted properly to the decision maker of the client, consultant or contracting organisation, preferably using that person's name. Further it must be attractive, informative and concise otherwise it will be 'binned' upon first glance.

Advertising may be done by in-house personnel or through marketing consultants – advertising agencies. The intent is to create a favourable image amongst potential customers (the decision takers in the markets). An important question is which media to use so that the advertising messages reach and are retained by the recipients. For such effective communication, it is best to use multi media, thereby achieving reinforcement of 'the message'.

Advertising is expensive, especially via television, and success is very difficult to measure; lags between advertising and responses may be long and varied permitting many other influence to occur. Hence it is important to set advertising objectives which are distinct (and as far as possible, measurable). Common objectives are:

- *branding* – establish a loyalty to the supplier
- *image building* – create a more favourable attitude amongst customers
- *education and provision of information* – tell customers what is available and what they may expect
- *changing attitudes* – persuading customers that they would be better off through consuming the advertised items
- *loyalty reinforcement and reminding* – retaining existing customers.

Due to the proliferation of clients who build only once or very occasionally, major repeating clients are valued highly by construction organisations and so are cultivated. However, the situation does mean that organisations must reach many customers to secure the necessary work – hence the importance of general advertising to make customers and their advisors aware of that organisation and what it can offer.

Basic advertising uses persuasion upon customers through 'method' – in which the characteristics of the service are sold, rather than the consequences of the service eg high quality factory built quickly and inexpensively, and/or 'personnel' – the reputation and experience of key people employed by the organisation which will translate into customer benefits, eg buildability expertise. The use of 'success story' approaches may be best for occasional/targetted advertising campaigns in which performance on, say, prestige projects can be employed, eg 'Nat. West. Tower'; 'Brooadgate'. Coverage, frequency and continuity are primary considerations in ensuring effective communication of the 'message' so that it is received, understood and acted upon whilst avoiding boredom and consequent resistance.

Often advertising budgets are set as £x per £ of sales; this 'rule of thumb' approach is used to set a 'norm'. The value of changes to the norm and of special campaigns, as already noted, may be difficult to assess. Information from sources such as interfirm comparisons will indicate how the particular organisation's avertising expenditure compares with others' and so can assist in gauging the success of campaigns (relative to their incremental costs).

Although bidding theory has now been developed to employ a utility approach, and so incorporate organisations various objectives, its basis remains price-oriented; particularly helpful as price remains the primary (if not the only) winner for construction projects. In the long period, an organisation must earn at least normal profits to survive; things are more flexible in the short period – hence the ability of organisations to 'buy' work. Estimating attempts to predict the costs to the contractor of executing a project; tendering or bidding is the process by which the contractor prices a project (usually based on an estimate). A somewhat 'grey' area exists between the two processes in which the costs to the contractor of such things as anticipated delay in receiving monies and 'market factors', eg desire to work with a major client, must be taken into account.

Estimating is not totally accurate, its accuracy can be judged only on projects which are won and, due to a myriad of difficulties, such judging is rare. However, research, eg ASHWORTH and SKITMORE, indicates that an accuracy (measured by coefficient of variation) of about 5% is normal.

As the objective of bidding is to submit the highest possible price to win the order and the estimate is 'known', the major variable is 'the market', ie the probability of the bid's being successful. The probability is assessed by reference to past performance and so feedback from tendering is essential. Bidding success rate is the major influence upon an organisation's cost of tendering which have been calculated to lie between a quarter of a per cent and just over one per cent of turnover.

The probability of a bid's success is obtained by comparing own bids on past, similar projects with the winning bid and the organisation's estimate. Obvious problems arise through changes in estimating accuracies, competition and market conditions. However, bidding models employ past success at the mark-ups used to predict the probability of success for the current bid (see, for example, FRIEDMAN (1956), GATES (1967), CARR (1982)).

FINE (1975) demonstrates the effect of estimating accuracy and level of competition on the mark-up required for an organisation to achieve break-even over many project bids and continues to provide a helpful mechanism for assessing how good the organisation has been at judging the market. By executing several trial calculations on past bids (knowing own estimate, own bid and the winning bid):

(a)   by applying a % mark up to each estimate, and
(b)   by multiplying each bid by a factor

and comparing the outcomes with what actually occurred through calculating the profit which would have/did result, then:

(i)   if (a) yields the highest profit, the organisation has judged the market badly
(ii) if (b) yields the highest profit, the organisation has judged the market quite well but has been pessimistic (if the factor is greater than 1).

7.5   Outputs

Image/Reputation

An organisation's reputation is derived from its outputs – what they are, their standards and how they have been produced, ie the processes of production used. An image is peoples' perception of an organisation and its outputs. Both image and reputation are employed to place an organisation in a hierarchy, ie how does the organisation measure up to its competitors? Other things being equal, an organisation will seek the best image and reputation but such enhancement may be expensive. As image and reputation (or aspects of them) can be poor or good, they act as 'losers' as well as 'winners'; thus poor aspects must be avoided, circumvented or got rid of as soon as they are detected. A bad reputation or image is far more damaging (duration, extent, ect) than a commensurately good one is helpful – damage is done rapidly and may be repaired only slowly and with much effort (due to customers' risk aversion).

The purpose of fostering a reputation and of creating an image is to generate enquiries and orders. For that to be achieved it is essential to know what the customers want, given what outputs and processes can be provided, and not just operate on the 'gut feelings' of the organisation's personnel. Research is important. BAKER (1985) found that 87% of customers selected the contractor by price, followed by (in order) company financial standing, company reputation, early completion date and prior business relationship; after price, contractors believed the order to be rather different and greater discrepancies were found to exist in some supplementary, less important criteria. Selective competitive tendering remains the most usual way of allocating construction work.

Thus, organisations would be well advised to foster a reputation, and to create an image, of providing the requisite outputs at a low price – the evident primary 'winner'.

Further, as pre-selection is usual, organisations should seek to establish a unique selling position (USP) for themselves in which their service or product is distinguished clearly from what competitors offer. Such may be achieved through selling by 'success story' – as epitomised by successful, prestige projects.

Apart from direct relations with customers, image is important in securing resources and retaining them. Many organisations foster the image of a trustworthy, family business which cares for its employees and gives them good training and job security. Not only is it an image of assistance in recruitment but it induces a feeling of stability amongst customers such that good performance is likely to be repeated through the organisation's having good, loyal, well-trained staff which are not 'lost' to other organisations once a project is completed, ie good performance is a stable and reliable expectation.

Enquiries
Enquiries are the initial indicators of likely marketing success – they are real opportunities to secure orders. A market oriented (rather than an output oriented) approach recognises that customers do not buy products or services but seek to obtain benefits, especially for producers' goods, eg industrial buildings.

Purchasing represents an amalagam of objective yardsticks (what is required? does the reputation of the organisation demonstrate that it will provide the required output?) and emotional experiences (the organisation's image).

Purchasing of buildings is almost never a repeat process – it is usually a new purchase or modified repurchase; the more extensive the 'new' elements, the more information and evaluation of alternatives which is required. As design is a lengthy process, normally separated from construction, there is a 'creeping commitment' of a client in procuring a building, choices are incremental. The situation does provide some scope for contractors to influence clients' choices between initial enquiry and placing an order.

To generate an enquiry (and then to seek its conversion into an order), an organisation should discover:

- who initiates an enquiry?
- who are the individuals involved in the relevant decision-making process(es)?
- on what bases will they decide about:
  (a) the service needed, and
  (b) who shall provide the service?
- what information do the decision makers require to reach a decision?

With repeating clients, there is likely to be a degree of buyer inertia – such risk reduction approach favours existing suppliers. The result is a margin of utility (price, reliability, etc) which is necessary to induce the buyer to (potentially) transfer from the existing supplier. Enquiries from such buyers may be little more than verifying that the existing supplier is acceptable but such enquiries do represent an opportunity for new suppliers to show their worth. To secure an order, the new supplier must:

(a) overcome the buyer's inertia to transfer, and
(b) offer the buyer sufficient margin of advantage to attract that buyer and so secure the order.

By the time an enquiry is formal as per single stage selective tendering, only price can be the winner; non-price advantages must have been demonstrated/exploited earlier in the work allocation procedure.

Orders

Orders represent the culmination of a cycle of marketing effort and the beginning of the next cycle. 'An organisation is as good as its last project.' Poor performance on one project, for whatever reason, especially if an important project, can reverse a vast amount of marketing effort – damage which may take a long time and much expense to repair.

Receipt of an order places the organisation in the position of buyer of resources to execute the project – labour, plant, materials and, notably, sub-contractors. Many primary sub-contractors (and suppliers) will be nominated or named to the contractor, thereby restricting the contractor's choice (and control?). For resources purchased domestically, contractors have considerable scope to exploit the competitive environments to their advantage – 'Dutch auctions' over sub-contracts have been notorious. However, as contractors' reputations, to a large degree, rest upon their sub-contractors' performances; there is much incentive to operate together for mutual benefits. Many contractors provide regular work to their preferred sub-contractors – mutual dependence is recognised and accepted.

7.6 Feedback

BELL found that 'experience' often was the only form of feedback in construction organisations – performance on one project was used in planning future projects and the organisation's marketing.

A formal system of feedback employs marketing audits. Such audits provide systematic, objective (critical and unbiased) appraisals of both the marketing environment and the organisation's marketing operations. The aims are to determine what the organisation's marketing objectives, strategies and actions should be and to identify potential improvements in the organisation's marketing. Audits should be regular, not 'fire-brigade', and should help to establish SWOT factors early. It is particularly important to identify 'winners' and to ensure that the organisation provides the necessary 'qualifiers'.

WILSON suggests four elements to be used as a test for a good marketing sub-system:

1 exercise tight, rapid and insightful control through accurate function definitions and realistic objectives
2 co-ordination; systematic and structured to encourage co-operation
3 information flows rapidly, accurately and regularly in both directions along communication channels, and
4 the structure can respond without distortion or fracture to internal and to environmental changes.

POWELL (1980) examined marketing of a variety of construction organisations and produced a marketing grid, shown as figure 7.6. The results do suggest that marketing in construction still has some considerable scope for development.

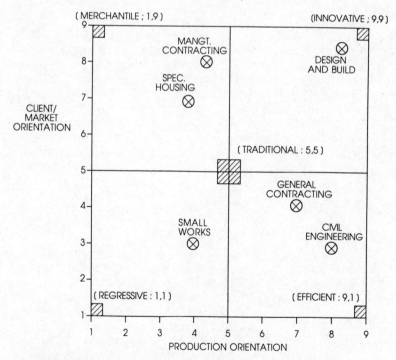

7.6 *Marketing grid*

Questions

1 Define the concept of 'market orientation' and discuss its significance to building organisations.

   CIOB *Building Management II*, 1988

2 The last decade has seen major changes in the marketing practices of private housebuilding firms.
   Discuss.

   CIOB *Building Management II* 1986

3 Compare the market research information likely to be sought by a speculative housebuilding company and a contracting company undertaking major industrial and commercial projects. Indicate reasons for any differences identified.

   CIOB *Building Management II* 1986

4 Describe and discuss the ingredients of a marketing plan. Evaluate the role of SWOT analysis in a building company's determination of the market sectors on which to concentrate.

References

Chapter 1
MILLER, E J and RICE, A K (1967), *Systems of Organization: The Control of Task and Sentient Boundaries*, Tavistock
OPEN UNIVERSITY (1974), People and Organizations DT 352 Unit 6: The Organization as a System, Open University Press.

Chapter 2
DEPARTMENT OF THE ENVIRONMENT (1987), *Housing and Construction Statistics*, HMSO
DEPARTMENT OF TRADE AND INDUSTRY (1986), Data Protection Act, HMSO
FELLOWS, F, LANGFORD, D, NEWCOMBE, R and URRY, S (1983), *Construction Management in Practice*, Longmans
FRYER, B (1985), *The Practice of Construction Management*, Collins
GHISELLI, E E (1973), 'The validity of aptitude tests in personnel selection', *Personnel Psychology*, 26, pp 461–477
LANGFORD, V and McDERMOTT, P (1984), *The sources, causes and effects of variations in Building Contracts*, Construction Study Unit, Brunel University, unpublished report
MEGGINSON, L (1981), *Personnel Management – a human resources approach*, Richard Irwin
MILKOVITCH, G and GRUECK, S (1985), *Personnel/Human resources management – a diagnostic approach*, Business Publications Inc
SCHMITT, N (1976) 'Social and Situational Determinants of Interview Decisions', *Personnel Psychology*, 29, No 1 pp 79–101

Chapter 3
INSTITUTE OF MATERIALS HANDLING (1965), *Introduction to Materials Management*
DAVIES, OWEN (1985), *Purchasing Management Handbook* chapter 1 'Purchasing Policy', Gower
LYSONS, C. K. (1981), 'Purchasing', M & E Handbooks
ILLINGWORTH, J and THAIN, K (1987), 'The Control of Materials and Waste' Technical Information Service Paper No 87
SKOYLES, E (1982), 'Materials control to avoid waste' *BRE Digest 259*, March

Chapter 4
HARRIS, F and McCAFFER, R (1982), *Construction Plant*, Granada Health and Safety Executive Transport Kills HMSO
MEAD, H T and MITCHELL, G L (1972), *Plant Hire for Building and Construction*, Butterworth
WINCH, G M (1985), *The Construction Process and the Contracting System Proceedings*, BISS

Chapter 5

COOKE, B and JEPSON W B (1979) *Cost and Financial Control for Construction Firms*, Macmillan

EDWARDS, J, KAY, J and MAYER C (1987), *The Economic Analysis of Accounting Profitability*, Oxford

FELLOWS, R F (1982), 'Some Aspects of Contractors' Cash Flow', Department of Building Technology, Brunel University, Working Paper No 21, April

FELLOWS, R F (1982) 'Cash Flow and Building Contractors', *The Quantity Surveyor*, September

FELLOWS, R F, LANGFORD D A, NEWCOMBE R and URRY S A (1982) *Construction Management in Practice*, Construction Press, November

FELLOWS, R F (1986) 'Escalation Management in the UK Building Industry,' *Proceedings CIB Congress*, Washington DC, pp 3857–3867

HOLMES, G and SUGDEN, A (1982), *Interpreting Company Reports and Accounts* (2nd edn), Woodhead–Faulkner

HUDSON, K W (1978), 'DHSS Expenditure Forecasting Model,' *Quantity Surveying Quarterly* 5, No 2 Spring

MERRETT, A J and SYKES, A (1975) *The Finance and Analysis of Capital Projects* (2nd edn), Longmans

SAMUELS, J M and WILKES, F M (1986) *Management of Company Finance* (4th edn), Von Nostrand Reinhold

SIZER, J (1979), *An Insight into Management Accounting* (2nd edn) Penguin

SIZER, J (1980), *Readings in Management Accounting*, Penguin

Chapter 6

BROMILOW, F (1974), 'Measurement and scheduling of construction time and cost performance in the building industry,' *The Chartered Builder* Vol 10

DEPARTMENT OF ENVIRONMENT (1971), *An information system for the construction industry*, HMSO

FRYER, B (1985), *The Practice of Construction Management*, Collins

GRAVES, F (1978), *Construction for industrial recovery*

HATCHETT, M (1971), 'Site Management – Time for a re-think' IOBA Site Management Information Service Paper No 41

HATCHETT, M (1976), 'The Elements of Supervision' *The Practice of Site Management*, ed P Harlow, CIOB

MOBBS, G N (1976), *Industrial investment – A case study in factory building*, Slough Estates Inst

NAOUM, S (1988), *An investigation into management contracting and traditional methods of building procurement*, PhD thesis, Brunel University

NEDO (1983), *Faster Building for Industry*, HMSO

NEDO (1987), Co-ordinated project information, Co-ordinating Committee for project information

ROWLINSON, S (1988), *An analysis of factors affecting project performance in industrial buildings*, unpublished PhD thesis Brunel University

TAVISTOCK INSTITUTE (1966), *Interdependence and Uncertainty*

TEMPORAL, R (1976), 'Supervisory Training in the Construction Industry,' *The Practice of Site Management*, ed P Harlow, CIOB

WOOD, K B (1975), *The public client and the construction industries*, NEDO

Chapter 7

ASHWORTH, A and SKITMORE, R M, *Accuracy in Estimating*, CIOB Occasional Paper No 27

BELL, R (1981), *Marketing and the Larger Construction Firm*, CIOB Occasional Paper No 22

BUTTON, K J (1985), 'New Approaches to the Regulation of Industry', *Royal Bank of Scotland Review*, No 158, pp 18–34 December

CARR, R I (1982), 'General Bidding Model', *Journal of the Construction Division* ASCE, CO4, pp 639–650 December

CHERNS, A B and BRYANT D T (1984), 'Studying the Client's Role in Construction Management', *Construction Management and Economics*, 2, pp 177–184

FELLOWS, R F, LANGFORD D A, NEWCOMBE, R and URRY S A (1983), *Construction Management in Practice*, Longmans

FINE, B (1975), 'Tendering Strategy' ed D A Turin, *Aspects of the Economics of Construction*, George Godwin

FRASER, W D (1984), *Principles of Property Investment and Pricing*, Macmillan

FRIEDMAN, L (1956), 'A Competitive Bidding Strategy', *Operations Research*, Vol 4, pp 104–112

GATES, M (1967), 'Bidding Strategies and Probabilities', *Journal of the Construction Division* ASCE, COI, pp 75–107, March

HARVEY, J (1987) *Urban Land Economics – The Economics of Real Property* (2nd edn), Macmillan

HILL, T (1985), *Manufacturing Strategy*, Macmillan

INSTITUTE OF MARKETING (1973), *Marketing in the Construction Industry*

LEVITT, T (1967), *Innovation in Marketing*, Pan Books, p 51

LIPSEY, R G (1979), *An Introduction to Positive Economics* (5th edn), Weidenfeld and Nicolson

MOORE, P G (1980), *Reason by Numbers*, Pelican

POWELL, N C (1980), *Marketing the Construction Service: A Review of Attitudes and Practice in the light of Increasing Environmental Uncertainty*, MSc disssertation, unpublished, University College, London, September

SEELEY, I H (1983), *Building Economics* (3rd edn), Macmillan

WILLS, G, CHEESE, J, KENNEDY, S and RUSHTON A (1984), *Introducing Marketing*, Pan

WILSON, A (1972), *The Marketing of Professional Services*, McGraw-Hill.

Index